T R A N S M O N T A N U S

A L L   P O S S I B L E   W O R L D S

Published by New Star Books
Series editor: Terry Glavin

All Possible Worlds

Utopian Experiments in British Columbia

Justine Brown

TRANSMONTANUS / NEW STAR BOOKS VANCOUVER

Contents

The residential school on
Kuper Island greets us
as we disembark.

I Remember Utopia

The Way Back

A GULF ISLAND HIPPIE COMMUNE, 1971, on an island so small, we wondered why it merited a ferry route. Yet as we disembarked on foot, scanning the wharf for our ride, we understood. Close by stood a colossal Indian residential school in Victorian red brick, one of the biggest in the province. Every window in the building was shattered, its walls scattered with scrawlings. With the exception of the commune, formerly a farm mission, Kuper Island is all reservation land. As the story went, the tribes of the area had long regarded the island as haunted. And it is tainted, daubed with bad blood – something that the utopians, mostly young Americans, were unaware of when they purchased the property.

But it was, in any case, irresistible – seafront farmland acreage, its pastoral fields and old fruit trees a source of comfort for those who found the coastal evergreen a little bit bleak, a little forbidding. It was often that way for the Californians who flocked to B.C. in the late 1960s to escape the draft and other less tangible threats. With its white wooden farmhouse and flower garden, its hay-filled barn, the property might have been Vermont. From certain angles, it might have been England,

Our parents planted gardens in the wilderness. Coastal B.C., 1970.

if you ignored the Indians across the island, the presence of an ancient burial site bordering the property, and the midden which was also our beach. For countless years, the natives had cast their shells there. Then, in the 1880s, the churchmen had come to build a stone mission by the sand. A huge oak tree, like the home of Robin Hood, overspread its arms there. And now the naked tawny hippie kids splashed and shrieked at the beach, sometimes clambering along the rocks to explore the skeletal remains of a fishboat wrecked decades before. In the woods adjoining the native burial grounds, our unwitting parents had built extra cabins and a geodesic dome which leaked in the rainiest months of February and March.

Were we oblivious, we children, to the phantom life of the island? I for one sensed the place to be crowded with ghosts. I experienced Kuper as gorgeous but troubled, and like a gorgeously troubled love affair, it lingers in memory. Trouble emanated from the restless dead. It sprang from the interracial tension on the island, which had an atrocity as its source: a government gunboat, questing for native pirates, had razed the village a century before. And trouble fairly radiated from the neurotic communards themselves. Ours was a fairly organized commune, a Gestalt therapy retreat founded by disciples of Fritz Perls. An earlier version had been located on an old motel site near Cowichan Lake on Vancouver Island; then came the split between Gestalt and the Primal Screamers, which brought our camp to Kuper. Some of the residents were permanent and some temporary, coming for a period of instruction, or working off hangups in the communal garden. We were all supposed to eat organic, and drink the pungent goat's milk. Trips to the supermarket at Chemainus, a ferry-ride away, were frowned upon. And nothing was more desirable. With its sexy enclosures of shapely, dependable edibles, nothing is more glamorous to a commune kid than junk food.

Jumbled together at random, we kids ran wild while our parents tried to recover in therapy the frankness and boldness they remembered from childhood. Childhood was imagined as invested with the truth of

Nature, before the candied edifice of civilized manners obscured it – the pavement of years. As a six-year-old, these adults seemed to me faintly disturbed, their emotions weighty in their faces as they struggled with the truth of words and gestures. They were forever confronting us with trivial matters: I resent the fact that you haven't finished your vegetables. I resent the fact that you left your dishes on the table. They refused to indulge in small talk, and deigned to respond only to "meaningful" words. Once, when the commune was in its final decline, I returned to Kuper for a visit. Only a few stragglers remained, living together in virtual silence. As we drove in from the ferry, past the residential school, down the green backroads, my comments went unanswered. They dropped through the air and landed on the floor of the truck: Wow. It's nice to see you. Boy. Spring has come to the island. Huh. Looks like that storm did some damage. So. How have things been? Thud, thud, thud … Gestalt speech was informed by a heavy theory of language, which equates literal content with meaning. The tentativeness of small talk is seen as meaningless, and light language – irony, playfulness – is reduced to the level of lies. I was never happy with these equations.

I remember utopia, though to remember utopia is paradoxical, since utopia has become yoked to the notion of futurity. Utopia is commonly understood as an ideal of future perfection. What I have learned in the course of my researches is this: utopia is a loaded word. For some people, it signifies "objectively perfect place." For most people, it means "naïve prescription for disaster." Approached about a book on utopianism, former commune dwellers typically recoil and become defensive. It is that word, utopia, that sets their teeth on edge. The world has come to jeer at their demolished dreams. Born in the 1960s, I seem to personify the sarcastic reproaches of those who came after.

Why has the word such a bitter, hollow ring today? The contemporary German philosopher Peter Sloterdijk remarks in his *Critique of Cynical Reason* that "after the decade of utopias and 'alternatives' [the 1960s] it is as if a naïve élan had suddenly been lost." We seem to be presented with a choice between earnest utopianism and cynicism, naïveté or clever irony. Must one exclude the other? Must we be *either* utopians *or* cynics? This opposition trips me, and I am landed back in the truck with the solemn, earnest hippie and his silence. It falls to those who came after to imagine a rueful, playful experimentalism – a half-smiling utopianism, which has learned something from its mistakes.

The etymology of the word utopia offers something to this project. The word was coined by Sir Thomas More, and plays on the Greek words *eutopos* (a good place) and *outopos* (no place). Playfulness is therefore inscribed into utopianism by definition. More's description of an imaginary island commonwealth in *Utopia* (1516) is a reflection on Plato's *Republic* as well as a satire on the laws of Renaissance England. Inasmuch as it describes an ideal society, it is a kind of secularization of the Heavenly Jerusalem of Revelations. Instead of pinning their hopes on the next world, European thinkers began to dream of perfection in this one. The neighbouring realms of Utopia and Eden actually overlap. The ideas are used almost interchangeably, and there is some justification for this. Eden is among other things a type of heaven: in the Bible, Eden foreshadows heaven (Paradise is synonymous with either or both). In heaven, we will regain what we lost with the Fall. And inasmuch as utopia is a secular version of the Heavenly Jerusalem, the place of perfection, it is like Eden.

But *Utopia* is also a parody travelogue — More modelled his text on the copious accounts of exploration which surfaced in the wake of the European discovery of America (the literal quest for the lost Garden of Eden is the predominant theme in these). And those who read the book simply as a prescription for the ideal society tend to skim over the jokey elements of the text, which undercut any such serious intent. Political science may be a descendant of *Utopia*, but so is the literature of fantasy and science fiction – the title of the book itself promises the description of a non-existent place. The narrator is called Hythloday, another Greek compound which means "expert in nonsense." A purely serious reading must also ignore the notes of ambivalence which punctuate Utopia.

More, who writes himself into the fiction, as a character, hears the story from Hythloday. While the description intrigues him, he feels uncertain:

> Meantime, while I can hardly agree with everything he said (though he is a man of unquestionable learning and enormous experience in human affairs), yet I freely confess that in the Utopian commonwealth there are many features that in our own societies I would like rather than expect to see.

II. PHANTASY GARDEN

… we read and hear little concerning it. The people in it are few, and the knowledge of it even less in proportion.

— Julian Ralph, describing British Columbia ("Canada's
El Dorado") in *On Canada's Frontier*, 1892

"THIS ISLAND IS LITTERED WITH FAILED UTOPIAS," remarks a character in Jack Hodgins' quintessentially British Columbian novel, *The Invention of the World*. What is true of Vancouver Island is true of the province as a whole. Not all of these communities need count as failures, however. An experimental period may rate as a success, and many are ongoing. B.C.'s utopian history begins well before Confederation, and extends well into the future. Even as I write this, several "intentional communities" are in the planning stages. Most of us can name one or two such experiments (Sointula, Brother Twelve's ill-fated Colony of Truth, etc.), but B.C. has produced hundreds of utopian communities, from the 1860s to the 1990s. This book is by no means an encyclopedia of B.C. utopias. It offers an overview.

The first utopian wave peaked between the world wars; the second wave peaked in about 1975, with an abundance of 1960s-inspired communes. Three government reports confirm our impressions with a raft of facts and figures – *The Alternative in Canada* (1973), *Something of Promise: The Canadian Communes* (1974) and *The Canadian Alternative* (1975). Compared with the United States, Canada as a whole has never been particularly rich in idealistic communities. Against the sparse backdrop of Canadian utopianism, B.C. is a glaring exception.[1]

A "utopian community" can be defined by its isolation, communalism and idealism, and also, perhaps, by an inclination to imagine everyday life differently. As often as not, communalism is the ideal that glues the group together. Sometimes, idealism overflows simple communalism. Generally speaking, the utopian community imagines itself, self-consciously, as an experiment. But occasionally it will spring up more fortuitously, anarchically, and this is a recurrent pattern in British Columbia culture. Our utopian impulses are clearly reflected in our literature, in novels like Hodgins' *The Invention of the World*, Audrey Thomas' *Intertidal Life*, Jane Rule's *The Young in One Another's Arms*, and even Douglas Coupland's *Shampoo Planet*.[2] B.C. culture, B.C. history – we are unused to thinking in these terms. This state of affairs is partly due to the fragmentary, fleeting, and self-effacing nature of B.C. history, which tends to be rumoured rather than known. Our ephemeral history seems to cover its own tracks at every step. No sooner does an event unfold than it is forgotten. The oblivion of local history is both a product of, and produces, the pervasive sense of British Columbia as nowhere.

"British Columbia" and "utopia" (no-place) intersect at nowhere. They coincide there. This nowhereness, mostly an accident of geography and of colonial patterns (it was the most remote and least populated of the British colonies), has long stood as a source of shame for B.C. intellectuals. The province has traditionally been the loser in the great Canadian race for identity. B.C.'s sense of place may have to rely, paradoxically, on the sense of no place at all. It is precisely this sense of nowhereness that has made the province so attractive for experimental thinkers.

Nowhereness has yet another source. Unlike the other provinces, B.C. joined Confederation in the absence of Indian treaties. This problem was swept under the carpet by politicians, who were anxious to close the deal, leaving B.C.'s legal status, in some respects, provisional at best. Often to the annoyance of native peoples and other permanent residents, outsiders have tended to imagine the region in terms of a vast emptiness, a blank page upon which to inscribe their fantasies. This is an attitude that ignores existent cultural patterns, but at the same time, it has contributed to the pervasive atmosphere of possibility which characterizes "the west beyond the west."[3] Though we may wander eastwards, we are drawn back to the place where we sense that anything may happen.

Sons and daughters of Abel, 1970, on the Sunshine Coast.

Geographically speaking, B.C. is a clearly defined space, enclosed by the Pacific Ocean, by the Rocky Mountains, by the cold, north country and by the United States drowsing fitfully to the south. This is the end of the line. Here, the exploratory impulse has painted itself into a corner – there is no place left to go. Eric Nicol writes that "British Columbians like to imagine themselves as a large body of land entirely surrounded by envy"[4] – shades of Milton's Satan patrolling the edges of Eden. It may be imagined as an enclosed garden, haunted by a phantom history, by its own fantasies; a "phantasy garden," in fact. This rich green landscape generates fantasy. This has long been the case.

At one level, this book represents an attempt to come to terms with the heritage of the 1960s. It is a heavily mythologized period, and a lot has been written about it, mostly by people who came of age then. The 1960s have been flattened, made entirely banal, by the popular media. My earliest memories date from 1968. I was three years old. My interest is not in the 1960s per se, but rather in what it means to come after that period, to be post-utopian. Mine is the perspective of the next generation, and is neither evangelical nor merely satirical. In talking to a lot of other people with a similar history, I have found that counterculture babies are remarkably ambivalent about the 1960s. They are nostalgic for idealism, excitement, newness, all things experienced at one remove. At the same time, they are critical of experimentalism and what it produced – in particular, sexual experimentalism. As the 1960s reached fever pitch, the nuclear family was declared null and void. Monogamy was under attack, and many parents tried "open relationships" with disastrous results. Families were shattered, and scattered to the four winds.

One thing the counterculture lacked was a sense of history. It emerged out of the repressiveness of postwar society, and it couldn't see beyond that. But before World War II – in the nineteenth century, at the turn of the century, between the world wars – there was a great deal of utopian activity. And just like 1960s experimentalism, it had mixed results. This is apparent in the history of B.C. utopias. The issue of free love, for example, created a lot of difficulty in Sointula, the Finnish colony on Malcolm Island. And there are practical lessons to be learned from, say, the Danes of Cape Scott. The problems of native/white relations were played out, to a large degree, at Metlakatla. And Brother Twelve's experiences show, among other things, the importance of maintaining a good relationship with the locals.

By placing 1960s utopianism in a larger context, we may be opening avenues for utopias of today and tomorrow. But one thing seems to me to be crucial in any such undertaking – a sense of fun.

Metlakatla

IMAGINE BRITISH COLUMBIA IN THE EARLY 1870s, its miles of dark bluegreen coastal forest unrolling northwards, with scarcely a dwelling to snag the panoptic gaze; scarcely a boat. To the European eye, this landscape epitomizes remoteness. Occasional Indian villages blend into the misty infinity of coastline as dusk falls over the Pacific.

Suddenly, half way to the Aleutians, a blinding glare of gas streetlights illuminates a crisscross of roadway. The villagers, about 1,000 Tsimshian people in dressy Victorian gear, are making their way home from evening prayers. The tall white church seats 1,200. Snatches of hymns can be heard circulating among the departing villagers. In the town square, a perfectly uniformed brass band, the pride of Metlakatla, strikes up a tune. From the church steps, a bearded and behatted white man surveys the scene possessively. He is William Duncan, Anglican lay minister, self-appointed saviour of the Tsimshian.

Wealthy English people on safari in the North Pacific liked to visit Metlakatla, which lay just adjacent to the Hudson's Bay Company trading post at Fort Simpson (now Prince Rupert). In Europe, Metlakatla was perhaps the best known place name on Canada's west coast. It was

The Metlakatla brass band poses before the town's massive church, 1860s.

a showpiece of "civilization." In Duncan's words, it was "a brilliant beacon light on the desolate Northwest coast, sending its splendid rays in all directions, the guiding star of all the heathen tribes." The community was eminently visible. To be visible was its raison d'être.

The light of Metlakatla inspired at least one other such community. In the 1880s, an Anglican missionary from Ireland, Robert Tomlinson, led a group of natives from Kitwanga, in Gitksan territory, to found a Christian utopia on the Skeena River, thirty miles downriver from Hazelton. It was called Meanskinish, but came, like Metlakatla, to be known as the "Holy City." Sarcastic passersby on the riverboats called it that because boats were not allowed to land there on Sundays.

Metlakatla's gas-lit streets of row houses were patrolled by a neatly outfitted native police force. It was well planted with flower gardens and fruit trees. Served by a co-operative store stocked with all the desirables from Victoria, the town featured a sawmill, tannery, soap and textile factory, printing presses, and a cannery. Its children had soccer fields and a playground with a merry-go-round. Its music lovers enjoyed the homegrown Handel choir, which performed *Messiah* all over the United States, displaying the transformative powers of Duncan's missionary fervour.

And transformation, for the Victorians, was the name of the game. The nineteenth-century missionary agenda reflected the widespread vulgarization of Darwin, valorizing a crude hierarchy. Europeans were seen to have competed their way to the top of the human heap, while "primitives" languished at the bottom. Now it was the missionaries' job to elevate everyone else.

Duncan's own metamorphosis parallels the dramatic mutation of the Tsimshian. He started small, the waifish son of a poor Yorkshire widow. Anomalous from the beginning, the pious infant William lamented the fact that his family members were "strangers to grace." Duncan's hard work and sparkling brain helped him ahead in the world. Most Yorkshiremen of his class wound up in the mills, but Duncan managed to get into the leather business, and with the help of a well-placed mentor he went from there to the Christian Missionary Society.

In 1857 Duncan found himself sailing into Fort Simpson (because the region was unnamed and virtually uncharted, Duncan was unable to get a life insurance policy before he left England; B.C. was legally nowhere). His mission was to remedy the damage done to the Tsimshian by the Hudson's Bay Company, with its liquor, guns, and crippling venereal disease. Some argue that he only succeeded in complicating the situation.

Duncan's account of his arrival is striking. As the ship sailed north, he had been gradually overtaken by dread. The landscape – grey, melancholy – moved by slowly, revealing more of the same. He caught an unfortunate glimpse of scattered body parts on the northern tip of Vancouver Island (probably Kwagewlth victims of a Haida war party). In a somewhat debilitated state, he reached the grand white turrets of Fort Simpson, around which teemed a masked and painted crowd. An odour of sulphur hung in the air, suggesting hellishness to him. Disembarking into the massed figures, Duncan felt the challenging glare of a handsome young Tsimshian chief. Legaic, the young chief, had by way of deft potlatching made himself the most powerful man among the Tsimshian. He wore an intricately carved head-dress and striped bandleader's trousers, but Duncan marched by without acknowledging him, marking the beginning of a convoluted relationship, one which tells us a great deal about his relations with the tribe as a whole.

The natives' position becomes clear via an exploration of different modes of power. Caught at the centre of a web of competition between various traders and missionaries, their first concern was to harness the power of the invaders. Duncan recognized the force of ritual in the natives' lives, and he was extremely wary of its power. This issue eventually lead to a breakdown of relations between the lay preacher and the Christian Missionary Society. Soon after joining the Tsimshian, Duncan wrote to the CMS that the natives were cannibals. He had witnessed this cannibalism first hand, he insisted, and his claim lent weight to his mission and brought in funds aplenty – the savages had to be civilized. Later, he admitted that what he had witnessed was only ritual cannibal-

ism, a kind of blooding. But given the metaphorical power of cannibalism in Tsimshian culture, it is unsurprising that Duncan, in his long association with them, consistently refused to give communion, or to allow it to be given in his church (the eucharist, after all, is a kind of ritual cannibalism – when we take communion, we eat the flesh and drink the blood of God made man). For this reason, it appears, he always refused ordination. Duncan felt keenly that the rite was too loud an echo of the kind of practise he was intent on abolishing.

Metlakatla in the 1860s. The colony sprang from a powerful mixture of Victorian and Tsimshian culture.

The day Duncan walked towards the gates of Fort Simpson, Legaic fixed the much-heralded new arrival in his gaze, trying to gauge Duncan's "spirit" (personal power). Legaic later made himself an ally of the missionary, donating a building for the mission school and sending along his own children for instruction. They arrived in face paint and spirit-dancing dress, thinking that receiving white power would be the same as receiving Tsimshian power. But when Legaic asked Duncan to close the school during a traditional initiation period for his daughter, the two men fell into conflict. Legaic claimed that the school activities would interfere with the power of the ritual. Duncan refused to close the school. He refused to compromise. Asked to at least stop ringing the bell, Duncan dug in his heels. Legaic confronted him, armed to the teeth, but backed down. It was a crucial moment in the dance of "powers." Legaic eventually converted and joined the exodus to Metlakatla.

What spurred the move? History brought colossal pressures to bear on the Tsimshian, and indeed upon B.C.'s entire native population, in the wake of the 1860s' gold rush, which lured untold thousands of whites into the province. The white population skyrocketed from a few hundred to about 35,000, and the white newcomers brought with them their own attitudes about native people. Victoria was transformed from a mud-streeted colonial outpost to a "fantasy boom town,"[1] boasting all the exotica it could muster. Whereas the fur traders had relied on good relations with the Indians – the source of pelts – gold-seekers maintained no dependence upon native people, and tended to view Indians as obstacles and lesser beings. The newcomers were notoriously abusive. Finally, 1862 brought a smallpox epidemic to the coast.

Given all this as a backdrop, it is easy to appreciate the attractions of refuge Duncan offered. Duncan had long planned to found a kind of Christian utopia. Now he seized his moment, casting himself as Moses, and investing the move with all the mythic power of the Israelite flight from Egypt. The chosen site lent itself gracefully to the chosen narrative: the Metlakatlan peninsula was the traditional winter home of the Fort Simpson Tsimshian, but had been abandoned for the riches of the trading post. An old chief, Neyastodoh, lent weight to the plan, telling Duncan, "If you want your people to be happy, you must take them to Metlakatla."

Only Christianized Indians were welcome in this New Jerusalem. Everyone had to agree to adhere to these rules:

> To cease calling in conjurers when sick
> To cease giving away property for display
> To attend religious instruction
> To send their children to the mission school
> To give up Indian deviltry

The rules reflect Duncan's primary task, which was to replace one system with another. The community was divided into ten "companies." Each company had its own colours and special metal badges, with the inscription "faith, love and loyalty" encircled with "United Brethren of Metlakatla." The model village would emblematize progress, a whole new ideology of work. It was a place where Indians would display their conversion from the potlatch system to one of individual accumulation, where they would display their conversion to the notion of progress itself, and abandon circular time for the straight trajectory of History.

Duncan has been vilified as a tyrant and a colonizer. But as Peter Murray points out in *The Devil and Mr. Duncan*, Duncan was sincere in his motives. He wanted to demonstrate that native people were "salvageable" within a colonial system, a system which, once it had abandoned the trade economy, was just as happy to be done with them altogether. There was a pervasive idea that the natives were incapable of change. Stripped of the economic power that trading brought, they would be no more than dangerous, bitter remnants of a crushed world. They were seen to pose a threat. But Duncan managed to dramatize, in Metlakatla, the fact that they could adapt if necessary. And however horrible that necessity was, it remains true that his policy saved a lot of people.

The Metlakatlans seem to have appreciated this. When Duncan was thrown out of the Christian Missionary Society, he was forced out of Metlakatla. Duncan and the Metlakatlans were too independent, too much themselves – too successful, in fact, for comfort. Finally, Duncan put his dreams for the Tsimshian ahead of the High Church itself. Metlakatla, originally a colony of the Anglican church, eventually gained its independence. Eighty per cent of the population followed Duncan to found New Metlakatla in Alaska, leaving behind all they had built, and all they had achieved, to take themselves forever out of B.C. territory. And out of ours.

Northern Lights

THE TURN OF THE CENTURY brought a wave of Scandinavian settlers to British Columbia. As the nineteenth century grew late, Norwegians, Danes, Finns, and others came west, establishing colonies that were informed, to varying degrees, by the spirit of utopian socialism. Utopian activity had intensified with time, particularly in the United States. Communities such as Brook Farm, a New England arts community, and Oneida, a highly organized free love experiment, sprang up as if in response to Marx's historical prophecies. The end of the century might coincide with the end of history, and the passage of time would naturally bring history to fruition in the form of a workers' paradise. For several singularly well-organized Nordic groups, the North Pacific became its designated location.

The first of these was a Norwegian colony at Bella Coola, followed by a settlement of Danes at Cape Scott, at the north end of Vancouver Island. The most famous was Sointula ("Place of Harmony"), a Finnish community formed on Malcolm Island in 1901. Each of these colonies was sufficiently united by idealism, sufficiently communal, and isolated enough to be described as utopian. Sointula was spectacularly so.

FACING PAGE: *The Bella Coola colonists on a recreational fishing expedition, 1890s. Finding little arable land in Bella Coola, many turned to fishing for their livelihood as well.*

There is an implied critique of the larger society in any intentionally isolated community. This is the opposite pattern to that of the company town, for example, in which the establishment of industry is followed by settlement. Here, idealism is the ordering principle, generally accompanied by only the vaguest of practical plans. In each case, however, utopian sensibilities played themselves out in a different manner.

The Bella Coola dream was born in a Minnesota schoolhouse in 1894. It was a cold midwestern night, and the Norwegian populace of Vineland, Polk County, assembled to hear the Reverend Christian Saugstad's account of his trip to Canada, where he proposed establishing a formal colony. The Rev. Saugstad, a Lutheran Free Church minister in a Lutheran community, was a captivating speaker. The weather had been particularly severe lately, he reminded the crowd, and the United States was in an economic slump. Farmers were poverty-stricken, and alcoholism was rampant. In Bella Coola they could start afresh. With its dark, evergreen fjords, Bella Coola was cast as a new Norway.

The original Bella Coola Colony Constitution, drawn up by the eighty-three founding members in the schoolhouse that night, is preserved in the collection of the B.C. Archives and Records Service. It is succinct and straightforward. The colony would be united by one preeminent rule: no booze. Breaking this rule would result in banishment: no exceptions. Prospective members had to furnish proof of "good moral character, working ability, and possession of means to cover travelling expenses and provisions for one year."[1] It was later decided that lots would be drawn for house sites, in order to minimize rivalry, and that staples would be purchased communally. The group interest would supercede individual interest.

The colonists – men, women, and children – left Victoria aboard the steamship *Princess Louise* in late 1894. One or two families had gone on ahead to make arrangements. They pitied poor Ole Oleson, who had got plastered and caused an embarrassing scene before the ship left port, leaving Ole to nurse his hangover in some nameless hotel, never to see the promised land.

Their first impressions of Bella Coola dramatized the implicit narrative of exile, salvation, and homecoming. At first, they felt rather scared. Enormous fog-wreathed mountains loomed all around, the steamship was surrounded by natives in canoes, and then, out of the mists, ten-year-old Bertha Thorsen appeared at the helm of a canoe, calling and waving, her blond hair whipping in the wind like a flag. This picture, an image of hope, stuck with the settlers. The first meeting of the Bella Coola colony was held on January 5, 1895, at Erick Nordschow's house.

The Norwegians, most of them farmers by trade, were dismayed by the absence of arable land. They immediately set to work clearing land, but were able to cultivate only the smallest of kitchen gardens. Most of them soon abandoned dreams of farming in favour of logging and fishing. Everyone worked together to put up buildings. In October, 1895, when the community celebrated its first wedding, between Kristian Karlsen and Miss Ovidia Baarli, it boasted numerous houses, a wagon road extending up the valley, bridges, a post office, a general store, and a library. The hall was beautifully decorated, and the choir performed a folk song specially composed for the occasion. All in all, the celebration worked to bind the community together. The experiment was deemed a success, and news of it spread back to Minnesota. Soon the *Princess Louise* returned carrying forty-nine new members. Two years after that wedding, Karlsen, the groom, was elected president of the colony.

In spite of its success, or perhaps because of it, the communal system gradually fell away. The colony dissolved smoothly into an ordinary town under a system of private ownership – the Bella Coola of today, in fact.

CONTEMPORARY BELLA COOLA stands in stark contrast to the utopian ghost town at Cape Scott, which is now part of a provincial park. It is still possible for hikers to see the vestiges of the Danish settlement that existed there from 1897 to 1909. The old communal building is quite well preserved, but some buildings are weathered down to their foundations. In the 1970s, an arsonist burned one of the houses to the ground.

Standing on the sandy beach, one feels what attracted the Danes to this particular spot of all spots. A lone Danish-American fisherman named Rasmus Hansen came across this enclosed lagoon in the early 1890s. Protected from the tempestuous weather, the lagoon was filled with halibut, ducks, and geese. Nearby was a clover-covered meadow, uncommon in that otherwise heavily forested area. The place seemed to beckon to him. He wrote of this "Shangri-la" in a Danish newspaper back in Nebraska, and received all kinds of letters in response. Together, the American Danes began to imagine an ideal Danish community in the remoteness of British Columbia. Experiencing the same depression that drove the Norwegians out of Minnesota, they focussed their hopes on unknown shores. The fantasy of a northwest paradise is tangible in the opening verses of "The Cape Scott Song," preserved in translation in the provincial archives:

> *Where the ocean waves pound on cliffs of old,*
> *Where the sun sets far on the ocean's floor,*
> *Where the leaning trees cast shadows bold,*
> *And deer disport on the sandy shore,*
> *Where Indians come, their food collected*
> *From the sea's stored wealth this sea food came,*
> *There is a land which for eons has waited*
> *For men strong and with courage to tame.*
>
> *Thus to a crowd Rasmus Hansen spake,*
> *To urge young men of Viking strain*
> *Dare you with me this long voyage take?*
> *Have you the will and courage to sustain?*
> *If so we can now this land possess,*
> *Slowly we will here an Eden make,*
> *And should Lady Luck grant us success,*
> *Then Cape Scott will reach a future great.*

This land, though it takes a lifetime's toil,
To make worthy for a future here,
And women may lack some city spoil
And work and weep and often despair
Now let us go to make good our claim
O'er ocean waves to this land at last,
And as comrades with one voice proclaim
Cape Scott, Cape Scott, we remain steadfast.

But Lady Luck never smiled on the Cape Scott community. The first twenty-five settlers arrived and set up a mill which was not particularly productive. They also built a dyke to protect the meadows from flooding tides, and a community hall was erected in 1900. The colony found unofficial leadership in Karl Brink Christiansen, known, by virtue of his education, as "the Professor." He is described as possessing natural authority and ability coupled with political know-how. Unfortunately, his writings were lost in a fire. It was near impossible to eke out a living at Cape Scott, and life was extremely difficult for the women in the isolated settlement, who had to perform their chores with very few amenities. The day they finished the dyke, a huge storm demolished it. A melancholy mood took hold of the place. The ultimate disaster came in 1909, when the CPR stopped serving them by boat. Disillusion, which so often rides tandem with idealism, produced its own anti-pastoral anthem by one Carl Chrisjensen, "Parody to the Cape Scott Song."

Where rain ever beats on distant shore,
Where sun fades behind the misty haze,
Where clouds drop their loads as they pass o'er,
And folk grope their way through the sticky maze,
Where Indians come their wood to get
From logs that drift on the reefs around,
There is a land. 'Tis best forgot
That Hansen saw, but he's no longer around.

To the crowd Rasmus Hansen spake,
To hear him men of all ages came
Dare you with me this voyage take
To seek this land in goodly frame
Endure the rain, mud, and sticky trail
As slowly is made attempt to drain
Lest plough sink deep and be of no avail
And all hopes of crops will prove in vain.

Always rolled oats your breakfast food
At night lard on bread was all to eat,
At mid-day a choice to suit your mind
From game, if lucky, or beans or meat
If from this food you can work extract
Whilst quenching your thirst on water brown
You will no doubt feel like an aristocrat
And on Indian maids no longer frown.

They followed him like a bunch of sheep
Though some would quit, some more would arrive
To stand in filth and dung kneetop deep
And somehow in this wetness did survive.
With brush they failed water to keep out
When the tides did rise and rain did fall
From flooding fields by dykes not stout
There's still room for many dare they call

'Tis on roads of slush we weary hike
And stagger along with seed to sow
Women drink tea they do not like
Instead of coffee they used to know
So now we are resolved to sever

Our life 'mid muck and cedar butts,
And seek high hills to stay forever
Cape Scott, Cape Scott, we now hate your guts.

NOT SO FAR FROM THE RAIN-SOAKED SHORES of Cape Scott lies Malcolm Island. Save for a hermit called Elliman (a Dane, coincidentally) and the occasional Kwagewlth clamming party,[2] it was uninhabited in 1900. A Christian sect of English and Irish people led by a preacher named Spencer had tried to establish a settlement there some years earlier, but poverty and infighting had made short work of their dreams. They had long since pulled up stakes, leaving only the faintest of traces. Unbeknownst to its sole occupant, Malcolm Island had just been designated the Finnish Utopia. The streets of Nanaimo's Finnish ghetto were ringing with good news. A saviour had appeared to lead them out of the slavery of the coal mines and into the socialist paradise.

Riddled with poverty and alcoholism, the Finns, like the Norwegians and Danes before them, felt themselves poised for change. They were sick of the mine owner, Premier James Dunsmuir, sick of the danger, and sick of the drink. They wanted a world of their own, a new life in the green seaside wilderness. All they needed was a virtuous leader. For some time the Temperance Society Lannen Rusko ("Western Glow") had been courting Matti Kurikka, a celebrated Finnish thinker living exiled in Australia, and finally he had agreed to come. They had to send $125 for his shipboard passage, for, as he wrote, he was "as poor as a churchmouse."

Matti Kurikka's arrival coincided with that of the new century. In Finnish intellectual circles, Kurikka was already a legendary figure, a passionate Tolstoyan socialist with all the appearances of a folk hero – tall, dark-eyed and soulful-looking, bearded, with long wavy hair. He radiated profundity. Kurikka had made a name for himself as a political writer, playwright, and editor. He championed the cause of the workers, women's rights (one of his teachers was Minna Canth, a well-known

Like the Metlakatlans before them, the Finns of Sointula were quick to organize an orchestra. Matti Kurikka is in the back row, fifth from right.

Finnish suffragette), and the peace movement. He denounced Russian imperialist tyranny and organized religion.

Upon reaching British Columbia, Kurikka instantly sent for his friend, Austin B. Makela, to aid him. He then founded a Finnish-language newspaper, *Aika* ("Time"), to promote his vision of isolated perfection. Its motto was "Freedom with Responsibility." Kurikka visited the various Scandinavian enclaves of British Columbia and Washington State, trying to excite interest in his utopian vision. In Sointula, he editorialized, "a high cultural life would be built, away from the priests who have defiled the high morals of Christianity, away from the churches that destroy peace, away from all the evils of the outside world."[3] Kurikka's notion of futurity drew paradoxically upon nostalgia for an imagined past. The enterprise would be named for Kaleva, a Finnish folk hero associated with the genesis of Finnish culture, hence the Kalevan Kansa

("People of Kaleva") Colonization Company. The name of Kaleva evoked a long-lost and misty ethnic ideality, now transposed onto a beckoning future. Here, Finnish culture would be reborn.

The purity of the wilderness was a cradle, Kurikka explained, which would nurture humanity's naturally positive impulses. Kurikka's gentle socialism, with its vague theosophical spirituality, is antithetical to Marx's philosophy of revolutionary violence. Kurikka's reliance, after Rousseau, upon inherent human goodness, aligns him with certain strands of anarchism. Kurikka foresaw change in terms of gradual conversion, rather than sudden violent upheaval, and Sointula would serve as an example: it would inspire a whole constellation of Sointulas, and eventually all of Canada would be absorbed into one harmonious collective.

The first group of settlers, five men, sailed from Nanaimo on December 6, 1901. During the voyage, a gun was accidentally fired and the captain, Johan Mikkelson, lost his thumb, and had to be put ashore at Alert Bay. Reaching Malcolm Island's Rough Bay eleven days later, the remaining colonists spent the night in the vestiges of Spencer's Christian utopia – a crumbling shack. They immediately set to work constructing a sauna; there being no organized religion on Sointula, the sauna all but replaced the church as the community's gathering place. By the time the second group of settlers arrived in January, the five men had managed to build a few log cabins.

Mrs. Wilander, the first woman in Sointula, cooked for the men and brought them coffee while they struggled away clearing trees. Work proceeded on two fronts: in the bush and on the pages of *Aika*, which was attracting Finnish immigrants from all over, and from all across the social spectrum. Coal miners came, but so did shoemakers, doctors, poets, theosophists, anarchists, and philosophers. There was a high turnover. About 2,000 people are thought to have visited the colony over a four-year period.

Each member was required to purchase a $200 share in the joint-stock company, but the poverty-stricken could exchange labour for shares. The colony was to support itself through logging, fishing, and farming.

Unfortunately, they had little experience of these things. Even as they completed the first community building, the Cedar Hall, they were already $1,300 in debt. This did little to discourage them, however. Excitement was in the air, and the curious streamed into Sointula.

In June, 1902, the community held a great celebration. A boatload of visitors arrived on the steamer *Capilano*. After the revels, the whole group assembled for a policy-making session around a colossal tree-stump, which served as a podium. Most of the visitors resolved to stay.

The Sointulans threw themselves into communal life. They took all their meals under one roof (drinking may have been done in private, however; like Bella Coola, Sointula was officially dry, but the colonists' descendants have excavated piles of liquor bottles dating from the turn of the century). All the food was prepared in the communal building – none of the cabins had kitchens. Everyone drew the same rate of pay ($1 a day plus food), but the number of hours worked depended on the nature of the job itself. Those with difficult jobs worked fewer hours. In their leisure hours, the Sointulans strove to fulfill Kurikka's harmonious vision of a "high cultural life," holding discussion groups, presenting plays, folk dancing, concerts, and choral music. A library was established in 1902 with the help of a group of Finns in Australia, who donated books and cash.

The community edifice was shaken to its foundations on a night in January, 1903. A fire destroyed the new meeting hall, which also served to house newly arrived families, killing eleven people. A large meeting was underway on the top storey that evening, and children had been left below. The islanders were discussing their multiplying financial problems, and were in the midst of a tricky debate when the cry of "Fire!" rang out. The stairwells were thick with smoke and flames. Women jumped from upper-storey windows, their hair and night-dresses ablaze, while others ran into the fire to save their children. Two women, one man, and eight children perished that night, and many more were injured. Austin Makela was badly burned, and nearly lost his eyesight.

An inquest team from Alert Bay determined that the fire had been an accident, not the rumoured work of an arsonist, but the rumour persisted nonetheless. It was whispered, rather illogically, that Kurikka, who some Sointulans suspected of embezzling the community's funds, had started the fire in order to destroy the colony's financial records. In retrospect, this seems unlikely. What is clear, however, is that Sointula's hopeful self-image perished with those children.

The colony tried to pull itself together. Plans were laid to build a large nursery, where women could leave their children while they went out to work, but the idea met with considerable resistance, as did most of Kurikka's initiatives concerning women. The community fabric began to unravel around the issue of "free love," which was one of Kurikka's favourite hobby horses. He filled the pages of *Aika* with his ramblings on the subject. "Marriage and love are two different things, just as the church and truth are two different things," he wrote. The fantasy of a utopian sex life challenged traditional ethical limits. Today the phrase "free love" conjures up visions of wholly unregulated sexual mores. In 1900, it simply signified sex without marriage. This idea in itself was explosive enough to seriously rattle the community, even developing into something of an international scandal when the newspapers picked it up. Although "free love" was never actually practised, Kurikka's writings left a strange impression. Because men outnumbered women two to one in the colony, monogamy was a touchy subject. A great deal of ill feeling was generated. Some of the men, who had wanted Sointula to be an all-male utopia, grumbled that women were nothing but trouble. And some of the women felt that Kurikka's ideas reflected badly on them – the world would assume that they practised "free love" (utopian communities are routinely discredited by sexual scandal).

Kurikka is remembered as a naïve dreamer. Unlike his colleague, Austin Makela, Kurikka came to be seen as unworldly and deeply unrealistic, a mystic. Makela leaned towards classical materialism. Another faultline appeared, this time between Kurikka supporters and Makela supporters. The final split came over Kurikka's disastrous economic policies.

School children celebrating May Day in Websters Corners, 1914. To fête the May Queen is also to fête International Workers Day.

The fire, which also destroyed $10,000 in buildings and equipment, left Sointula in financial crisis. In 1904, Kurikka bid for and was awarded a contract in North Vancouver under which the colony would supply the lumber and the labour to build bridges over the Capilano and North Seymour rivers. Everyone agreed that the bid was far too low, and the colony lost a great deal of money. Kurikka departed in a cloud of acrimony, taking about half the settlers with him to Vancouver. The trip took about two weeks. Shortly thereafter, the Kalevan Kansa Colonization Company was dissolved.

While the Malcolm Islanders regrouped themselves, Kurikka's exhausted supporters moved into a hotel in Vancouver's Chinatown. Kurikka himself moved into the colony's nearby former offices and raised chickens in the basement. In 1905 he inaugurated a new colony at Websters Corners, near Maple Ridge. Women were deemed to be a subversive presence: Sammon Takojat (Haven of the Sampo, a magical mill), a.k.a. Sampola, was an all-male community. Kurikka wrote to a friend that all "the best men" of Sointula had joined him. Like theosophist monks, all twenty-four of them worked together making shingles, and slept together in one large room. Soon tiring of this, they bought a nearby farm, built saunas, and readmitted women. Bachelors married, and husbands were rejoined by their families. A school was opened.

Kurikka departed for Finland, then went to the United States, and spent the remainder of his life campaigning tirelessly for Finnish sovereignty, although he never fully abandoned the utopian landscape. A late photograph taken in his Connecticut study shows Kurikka surrounded by books and papers. Bearded and bespectacled, he frowns into the distance, squinting, perhaps, at the past, and the bright glare of its northern lights.

Prospero's Islands

Had I plantation of this isle, my lord ...
And were the King on't, what would I do? ...
All things in common Nature should produce
Without sweat or endeavour ...

– Shakespeare, *The Tempest* II.i.

Daddy used to tell me there was a black magician on one of the islands
around here, practising evil rites ...

– Malcolm Lowry, *October Ferry to Gabriola*

ANY HISTORY OF UTOPIAS necessarily includes a sub-history of charismatic leaders. Indeed, it is frequently argued in the literature that the
only "successful" utopian communities are those guided by a single,
magically seductive personality. A sound economic base, a unifying collective philosophy, a charismatic leader – these are held to be the elements of a workable (read enduring) utopia. The main protagonist of
Jack Hodgins' novel *The Invention of the World* represents a collage of
B.C.'s utopian kings. Hodgins' Donal Keneally, like the similarly

Aquarian children preparing
a pageant celebrating spring.
Note the fern costume, third
from left.

named Matti Kurikka, is the magnetic leader of an ethnically homogeneous colony. Also like Kurikka, Keneally's powers of sorcery derive partly from the mythically charged accounts of his birth, which invest him with the glamour and clout of an ancient hero. Born out of the union of an Irishwoman and a bull, he boasts all the bull's cartoonish virility. After a bewitching magic show, Keneally leads a whole village out of Ireland and into the promised nowhereland of Vancouver Island.

Keneally resembles Kurikka, certainly. But he resembles the notorious Brother Twelve even more. Brother Twelve, a.k.a. Edward Arthur Wilson, led a group of wealthy and influential people to found his ill-starred Colony of Truth on an island off Nanaimo in 1927. Conflicting stories about Brother Twelve proliferate, and it is virtually impossible to pin down the facts. What is more interesting than stable facts, however, is the degree to which Twelve has been mythologized in British Columbia.

He was a magician in a manner which blurs the distinction between the present-day meaning of the word (i.e., illusionist) and the Renaissance meaning, which implies genuine sorcery. According to one tradition, Wilson began his adult life as a carny, a circus traveller of a type that proliferated in the period between the wars.[1] Like the Kansas alterego of the Wizard of Oz, the turbaned swami in the caravan, Wilson travelled North America telling fortunes. Like Magnus Eisengrim of *Fifth Business* fame, he became skilled in performative magic.

His origins are suitably shrouded in mystery. He was probably born in England in 1871, although some accounts make him a Canadian, and others have him as an American. He liked to tell the credulous that he was the son of a Brahmin princess. His appearance – rather dark-skinned, slim, bearded, with piercing eyes – reinforced this fairytale. He may have run off with the circus at an early age. He also worked on ships, and it was a ship that first brought him near Vancouver.

Wilson was a disciple of the theosophist Madame Blavatsky, denizen of the spirit world, and he was a member of the Great White Lodge, Blavatsky's esoteric society. Wilson has been placed in Genoa during the time the notorious Aleister Crowley lived there, and it seems likely that Wilson knew Crowley. It was during this time he fashioned his Brother Twelve persona (or, more precisely, "the Brother, Twelve"), and began drawing a crowd of followers about him. Silent film stars, bankers, playboys, and purseholders of all kinds thronged to see Wilson "channel" Brother Twelve, who was touted as an emissary from his eleven intergalactic brothers. They hailed from the planet Aquarius. People were hungry for answers in the turbulent years between the wars, and apocalyptic philosophies flew thick and fast in the cultural climate typified by Weimar, so neatly evoked in the novels of Christopher Isherwood. Peter Sloterdijk may be right in comparing the 1920s to our own period. All over the Western world, people were questing for bandwagons to jump on. The air was heavy with imminence, as though a long-awaited storm was about to break. The apocalyptic mood represents an intensification of history, History with a capital H: the sense of being on the verge of an unavoidable Something Big. People found the answer in communism, fascism and other authoritarianisms. One coterie of two hundred found it in Brother Twelve's doomsday philosophy.

The message from Aquarius was this: after a period of extreme economic chaos, turning civilization upside down, the world would end on January 1, 1934. Great wars would ravage our planet, but, assured the Brother, Vancouver Island and environs would be spared. The chosen few were to gather there to await the end of the known world, at which point they would usher in the Age of Aquarius and live for a thousand years. They were to pool their abundant cash and build an ideal community on De Courcy Island. Of one accord, the Aquarians made their way to the edge of the world.[2]

It is remarkable how well the islanded coast of British Columbia lends itself to this kind of program. Under Brother Twelve's magical gaze, this isolated nowhereness, this no-place, would suddenly become the only place on earth. As B.C.'s sorcerers have always intuited, deserted islands lend themselves wonderfully well to enchantment. A good part of Prospero's wizardry in Shakespeare's *Tempest* derives from the sense of enclosure, of kingdom, that only an island can offer. Prospero, a sorcerer-ruler, has complete control of his encircled subjects. In this connection, it is well worth noting the profound confluence between *The Tempest* and *Utopia*. Both are Renaissance island narratives, in some sense engendered by the discovery of the New World. Both are partially modelled on the kind of travelogue that sprang from the age of exploration. Like *Robinson Crusoe*, *The Tempest* contains many references to a real-life desert island story. Gonzalo's speech ("Had I plantation of this isle, my lord, and were the King on't, what would I do?") is an explicit meditation upon Utopia. Indeed, by the seventeenth century, imagining one's own personal utopia had become a kind of parlour game.

The fantasy of island life is a fantasy of freedom, of being able to order things exactly as one likes. From the community of expatriate American blacks who settled on Saltspring Island in the nineteenth century, through to the still-thriving Shire of Hornby, the Gulf Islands are loaded with utopian culture. So many are the communal experiments on the Gulf Islands over the years that they form, to my mind, a virtual utopian archipelago.[3]

Brother Twelve's Colony of Truth is a kind of model, however sinister, and Twelve himself an archetype of B.C. history, his example resonating in various communal leaders even as I write this. Rumours about Brother Twelve still echo down the years, and each new journalistic exposé only strengthens his mystique. This is precisely what "the Brother," whose whole stock in trade was mystification, would have wanted. Seduction, murder, magic, buried gold and munitions; a celebrated escape – to retell his story is to weave a tissue of rumour.

In a 1967 potboiler, apparently written in response to the renewed interest in the occult, a man claiming to be Wilson's natural brother unfolds a fantastical story. It appears that the colonists arrived near Nanaimo in the spring of 1927. Brother Twelve led them, accompanied by his common-law wife, a devotee named Elma. The first settlement of the Aquarian Foundation was at Cedar-by-the-Sea. With a cash infusion from Mary Connally, a Southern socialite, Brother Twelve was able to buy the islands of Valdes, De Courcy, and Ruxton, where further settlements went up. Among the colonists was a German aristocrat, Maurice von Platen, an American ex-secret service agent, and a Californian novelist. Unaccustomed though they were to manual labour, they set to work, and had soon planted a garden and helped build forty-six cabins that encircled the leader's House of Mystery. Apart from the occasional shopping trip to Chemainus, they kept to themselves. Affecting the Christlike garb of a carpenter, Brother Twelve wandered among them, overseeing the whole operation.

Once his kingdom had been built, he turned his attention outwards. He recruited a printer and began circulating a promotional newsletter, *The Chalice* ("Herald of the New Age"), then went on a fundraising drive through the United States. Money rained onto the Colony of Truth, and Brother Twelve, a.k.a. "Guru," soon deified himself. He then appointed a number of High Priestesses, and performed intricate nighttime rituals on the beach before the assembled community. One of these rites was witnessed by passing fishermen, and the wrath of the locals was aroused as word got around that the Aquarians were having orgies on the beach.

At the centre of the group of priestesses was a young woman, Myrtle Baumgartner. She was supposed to be a reincarnation of the Egyptian goddess Isis, while Brother Twelve was Osiris. In the role of sacred prostitute, she had been appointed to bear the Brother's Christ-child. But the Brother's authority was radically undermined when Myrtle miscarried the promised saviour boy. After a second miscarriage, Myrtle suffered a nervous collapse and went mad.

Some of the colonists resented the Brother's fornicating with Myrtle in the House of Mystery, and doubts began to circulate in the community. Things went from bad to worse when a few of the colonists charged their leader with embezzlement of funds, which led to the Colony's first mutiny. Brother Twelve was brought to trial in Nanaimo in 1928, but the case came to nothing. Before the outraged citizenry, the sorcerer was released. The reason – he appeared to have hypnotized the witnesses. The newspaper accounts describe them, fixed in the Brother's inescap-

able gaze, gibbering and falling to the ground in the midst of testimony. Judge Barker, when he tried to speak, growled like a dog. Some said that Twelve released ampoules of noxious gas, concealed under his shirt, into the courtroom. With some of the chastened rebels in tow, Twelve returned to his island in triumph.

Newly invested with power, he was newly power-hungry, newly sadistic. He began converting Foundation funds into gold coins, and instructed an assistant to store the gold in quart mason jars and sink them into the cistern of the main house at Cedar. He then began collecting arms, and built five forts around his home on De Courcy.

Myrtle was replaced by a surly newcomer, a thin, black-haired dominatrix called Madame Zee. Madame Zee had come out from Florida with her third husband, a long-haired stage hypnotist and poultry millionaire ("Florida's poultry king") named Roger Painter. When Zee began visiting Twelve's cabin at night, Painter flew into a violent rage and left the colony. Having driven out Zee's husband, Twelve pro-

The colonists relax in one of their hand-built structures. Brother Twelve is shown in profile at the right.

ceeded to get rid of Myrtle. Rumour has it that he murdered her and made a finger bowl from her skull. Twelve claimed that his Isis had returned to her home town, but a later investigation of the House of Mystery did turn up a bowl made from a human skull. Forensic tests showed that it belonged to a woman about twenty-five years old.

By this time, the colonists, like sailors under a Circean spell, were metamorphosed into slaves. Twelve and Zee transformed themselves as well – Twelve renamed himself, aristocratically, Amiel de Valdes, and he then announced that Zee was a god as well. The two travelled to England in high style, where they bought a yacht, the *Lady Royal*, and sailed back to British Columbia via the Caribbean and South America.

Upon returning, the newly deified Madame Zee strode around in modified S/M gear, whipping the islanders as they sweated over the vegetable gardens. As part of a test, one old woman was pushed to the brink of death. One source reports that, Oz-like as ever, Brother Twelve miked the main compound, eavesdropping on the colonists and projecting voices around.[4] There was a rigid hierarchy in place – Cedar was for the merely interested, Valdes Island for disciples, De Courcy Island for the inner circle, and Ruxton Island, "the Devil's Island," served as the jail.

In 1934, the world failed to end as predicted. Mutinous murmurings began to percolate once more, and a violent struggle broke out. The colonists fled for Nanaimo. Meanwhile, Twelve and Zee destroyed as much of the compound as they could, razing fruit trees and blowing up outbuildings before fleeing on their private boat with as much wealth as they could carry. They made a stop at Roberts Creek, across the Strait of Georgia on the Sechelt Peninsula, then disappeared. They were never apprehended.

Twelve reportedly died in Switzerland soon after, but his death may well have been faked – several ex-disciples report having contact with him in the years that followed. One of them, Philip Fisher, a manic depressive affectionately known as "the Nut," tried to start another theosophical commune, the City of Light, in the hills behind Chemainus. He petitioned the town council, playing them strange tape-recordings from "the Masters," who allegedly governed planetary affairs, but Fisher's City of Light was never developed beyond the gates of his own imagination.

IN MAY, 1967, THE WEST COAST was gearing up for an unforgettable summer. Herbert Wilson had just published *Canada's False Prophet: The Notorious Brother XII*, and it was causing quite a stir, dovetailing neatly with the dawning of the Age of Aquarius. On the Gulf Islands, shades of Twelve were soon flitting through the damp undergrowth. Lasqueti residents began to feel uneasy – another "messianic nut" had appeared on the scene. It was whispered that Ted Sideras prayed to the rising sun, and that he lived in a sort of castle filled with secret passage-ways, filled in their turn with draft dodgers and teenage runaways; that he had thrown up seven-foot battlements around the property to conceal orgies. His mysteriously acquired riches were converted into gold bullion. He and his followers were said to be armed to the teeth.

By 1970 the whispers had reached the Ontario offices of *Maclean's* magazine, which dispatched a reporter to investigate "Canada's commune country." Allan Edmonds' article came out soon after. In 1991, Edmonds wrote a follow-up article. The two articles form a diptych of hope and disillusion, evocative of the melancholy which followed close on the heels of 1960s idealism.[5] In 1970, Edmonds came away from Lasqueti highly impressed with Sideras and his "family." Later, in the aftermath of a scandal that broke up the commune, he was asking himself how he could have failed to detect the warning signs when he visited "Sideras Place."

Edmonds learned that the American-born Sideras had come to B.C. with his friend, George Orton, together with their wives and children, from Oregon. In a now-familiar drop-out pattern, the discontented middle-aged twosome had sold their lucrative businesses (a restaurant, an employment agency, and a credit-reporting bureau) with a view to starting life afresh in the wilderness. They bought eighty acres on Lasqueti and pitched camp there. Gradually, news of Sideras Place crept through the "hippie underground" and a tent hamlet spread into a tent village, population 50. Among them were anthropologists, sociologists, a lithographer, a welder, and a dress designer. A woman with a doctoral degree in education home-schooled the children. William Deverell, the lawyer-turned-novelist, advised them, and was a frequent visitor (Deverell's book *The Dance of Shiva* was inspired by Sideras Place). No-one among them knew much about construction, but they managed to build the main house, described by Edmonds as "a massive schloss-like mansion of stone, roofed and half-panelled with hand-split shingles or shakes."

Edmonds liked Sideras, who reminded him of Woody Allen. The photographs depict a decidedly un-rugged figure, lightly bearded and heavily bespectacled with thick black-framed glasses, his quintessentially mid-1960s hair plastered toupee-like across a huge forehead. Clad in a dark overcoat, he stands smiling on a bluff. Another photo shows him discoursing at the dinner table. Sideras loved to rap. Everyone recalls his magic tongue. He loved to hold forth, philosophizing in the time-honoured anti-philosophy tradition ("What's philosophy? ... a category, and to us there aren't any"). He was strangely charismatic, but seemingly uncoercive.

Nobody was forced to do anything, and anyone was free to visit. Anarchist-style, the commune was self-organizing. It was financed by the founders, with occasional donations from new members. Sideras' own notion of indefinability is paradoxically definitive of no-place utopianism: "This life is like gossamer," he said, describing the commune, "when you try to touch it, it vanishes." In a nicely *outopian* (no-place) gesture, Edmonds declined to mention the exact location of Sideras Place in his article. But this only served to increase public curiosity, and the commune was soon deluged with letters and visitors. Perhaps as a result of his new notoriety, Sideras became more guru-like.

Commune dwellers were asked to leave their identities at the gate. The past was to be forgotten. Only the future was real. Books, artefacts of the outside world, were frowned upon, and making music was forbidden. Sideras promoted a ritual known as the Asking, which involved wandering out into the forest for an unmediated session with God. Ask God, or "Papa," for the answers, said Ted. At first the answers were pretty abstract. But as the commune drifted into financial straits, and the pressures of feeding so many people grew more overwhelming, the answers became increasingly practical. Soon Papa instructed Sideras to start rustling cattle.

WITNESS SAYS GOD OKAYED CATTLE KILLING, reads the headline. Sideras and Orton were brought to trial at nearby Qualicum Beach, on Vancouver Island, in 1972. Commune dwellers testified that Sideras had passed on instructions from God to butcher a neighbour's cows. The trial lasted a long time, and although the judge recognized that some thirty-five cows had been killed, the charges were dismissed for lack of concrete evidence. Meanwhile, Sideras' charisma was backfiring again. Don McPherson, the father of a commune dweller, phoned Sideras and accused him of brainwashing his son. "I'm going to get you, you son of a bitch," he told Sideras, who decided to take him at his word, and charged McPherson with threatening his life.

Under siege, the commune moved north, from Lasqueti Island to Calvert Island. The family had grown to about eighty people, but morale had collapsed. Food was scarce, and blackflies were plentiful. It rained all the time. Ted was immobilized by depression and paranoia. Members recall that the community bristled with guns and knives. There was an armed confrontation with some hunters. One young man cracked up and ended up in hospital. Half-finished structures, inspired by sunnier days, moldered in the rain. As the community unravelled, Sideras sat dreaming in his tent. As the rain streamed on the roof, he had an idea. This melancholy, the mood of the new decade – maybe it was the weather. Damn this wet. Before him hovered a new vision of paradise: Fiji. To hell with the rainforest. And to heaven with the family. He emerged from his tent, and led all who would follow to the South Pacific. When he was last heard from, he was living in Fiji with his wife and kids.

B.C.'S UTOPIAN KINGS RISE AND FALL rhythmically through time. Often outsiders, drawn by news of warm weather and empty space, they come to stake a claim in dreamland. Brought down by the damp, by internal dissension and the threats of the locals, they retreat.

In the late 1980s, the Gulf Island rumour mill was churning once more, this time over an obscure group of Spanish polygamists that arrived on Mayne Island in 1986 – seven Spanish women, short-haired and dark-eyed, and a mysterious cult leader called Father Ivan, who had sired most of their fifteen children. Local shopowners found them polite but secretive. A foul odour rose from their dilapidated compound. Their goats rampaged through the neighbourhood. Their attempts at fish-farming were disastrous. They made abortive attempts at logging their land, and left great piles of valuable wood to rot in the rain. Apparently they could afford to. The Spaniards had a swimming pool, but no visible means of support, and as their children proliferated from fifteen to twenty-nine, people began to talk of babyfarming instead. Or maybe they were running drugs up and down the coast. Pressed for answers, the Spaniards began generating religious ikons for sale abroad. This was their means of support, they said.[6]

Central to the story of "the Spanish sex cult" is one of the longest-running refugee claims in Canadian immigration history. By 1994, the Spaniards had made more court appearances than Brother Twelve and Ted Sideras put together. Father Ivan himself, however, generally managed to remain invisible. The group frequently starred in Moira Farrow's shock-horror immigration articles in the *Vancouver Sun*, but the combined efforts of several investigative reporters shed little light on its leader. Just as God in a Madonna-and-child portrait is made conspicuous by His absence, so Father Ivan, a.k.a. Pedro Vivancos, is made conspicuous by his. It was alleged harassment by their Roman Catholic neighbours back in Spain (the basis of their humanitarian-grounds refugee claim) that provoked the departure of Father Ivan and his Vivancas to Montreal in 1984. In Canada, four of the seven women married Spanish-born Canadian men. Their religion, which is apparently

Two Vivancas deter
journalists at the gate of
their Rock Creek compound.

based loosely on Sufism, embraces a tradition of monasticism without celibacy – hence the emphasis on communal isolation. Finding Montreal cold and ill-adapted to their purposes, the group made its way to the B.C. coast, reputedly a warm and tolerant place. They settled on Mayne Island, intending to start a school for their abundant offspring.

The group's focus on children is common among such communities, where utopianism translates as an exploration of human potential. Several B.C. communes, including one on Lasqueti and one near Lund, north of Powell River, have been founded with the stated aim of starting an alternative school. In an informal school, the Spaniards' children studied French, Italian, English, Spanish, and Chinese. They were well-versed in music theory and world history, and began travelling to Vancouver for ballet lessons as well. The group philosophy was non-coercive: when the kids wanted to dig clams, they dug clams. After four uneasy years on Mayne Island, when the Vivancos failed to get permission to build a properly registered independent school, they moved to Rock Creek in the southern B.C. Interior, and founded a school called

Quanticoh. Their mere presence appears to have alienated all their new neighbours, mostly cattle ranchers.

Quanticoh made a bizarre collective appearance in September, 1991, on a Canadian Airlines flight to Mexico. Presenting themselves as schoolteachers, six Vivancas boarded the airplane with all the children, whose numbers had by now swelled to forty-three. The school was on an outing to Mexico – squalling babies, toddlers, teenagers and all. The Vivancas shocked airline employees by refusing all refreshment, including soda pop and salted nuts. They had brought food for everyone. When they missed a connecting flight in Los Angeles, the airline took pity on this travelling circus of fifty or so and put them up for the night. Catching wind of the exodus, the immigration authorities were relieved. But they had not seen the last of the Spaniards. Not nearly. Mexico did not prove to be the perfectly tolerant, perfectly oblivious place they desired. Slowly, they trickled back into Canada.

In 1994, the magically elusive Father Ivan was arrested on immigration charges in an apartment near the Burrard Street bridge, where he was staying with two Vivancas. They all appeared in court, and were released pending another hearing, while their lawyer sought to exclude the press. The Vivancos want invisibility. But they are learning what Brother Twelve and Ted Sideras learned before them – the mere desire for isolation produces its opposite. Father Ivan is right to be elusive. Time and again, history has shown that the power of a "cult" leader depends upon mystery.

Spirit Wrestlers

AN OLD FRIEND OF MINE grew up on a commune near New Denver, in the Kootenays. Born in August, 1967, in the heat of the Summer of Love, he remembers the West Kootenay and its overlapping spheres of utopianism. Utopia refracted through his childhood experience. Between the numerous hippie communes and the traces of earlier experiments, the West Kootenay was like a hall of mirrors.

His parents, earnest American youngsters, had arrived in the Canadian forest with the first wave of back-to-the-landers. Clutching their copies of *How to Build Your Home in the Woods*, they cleared the land with axe and chainsaw. Soon, an A-frame colony flourished on the hillside, a communal kitchen garden in its midst. Yellowy-orange marigolds shone among the carrots, the tomatoes, and the burgeoning zucchini. Someone had dressed the scarecrow in rainbow colours. While the adults happily gardened in the nude, burnished and unkempt, the commune kids, de facto siblings, went to the local school by riotous schoolbus. At school, they had to contend with the jeers of the locals: you stupid *hippies*. I saw your folks *naked*. And this in the Kootenays, where, unbeknownst to the American newcomers, zealous Doukhobors had

Not nudists of the 1960s, but
Sons of Freedom protesters
circa 1908.

been parading nude routinely for at least half a century.

The hippie enclosures bordered closely on Doukhobor properties. Those were turbulent days. The Sons of Freedom, a Doukhobor sect, were constantly making headlines. Firebombed houses burned and naked Freedomite women, heavy and sombre, stood in silent reproach against materialism and other enemies. They felt no need to speak. The Edenic gesture would proclaim their innocence. But in the eyes of a six-year-old, long-haired boy, passing them on the flatbed of his parents' gaily painted hippie pickup truck, a relic of Depression days, these other nudists were opaque, shrouded in mystery. He was puzzled by the sight of the naked Russians, and he was puzzled by their long-abandoned communal brick houses, their yards and orchards overrun with weeds.

Hippie communards found themselves haunted by these utopian ghost-towns, which boded ill for the future. Another strange spectre in New Denver was the dystopian ghost-camp of Japanese internment, itself set up in one of the ghost-towns that riddle British Columbia as a function of our resource-extraction economy. In this case, the government found some use for them – housing Japanese internees – and the evacuee villages present an inversion of utopian community, a looking-glass world. Such places negate utopian freedom. Instead of freely choosing to go and live communally in the name of human potential, you are forced to go and live communally because of a presupposed potential for evil.

Both hippie nudity and Doukhobor nudity announced Edenic innocence and anti-materialism. Both alienated mainstream society. But the Doukhobor gesture was historically coded in ways which were unintelligible to most, including the six-year-old hippie kid, himself a marginalized figure in the post-1960s days of "us and them" (longhairs vs. crew-cuts, patriotism vs. pacifism, etc.). Mention the word "Doukhobor" and many British Columbians will snicker. The word instantly conjures up visions of naked fanatics.[1] This nudity has a long history: a Vancouver journalist notes in 1914 that the Russian immigrants were "occasionally a nuisance to police because they sometimes appear on the street without any clothing." In fact, the protests were carried out by a dissident

Doukhobor sect, the Svobodniki, or Sons of Freedom, which became prominent after the Doukhobors' 1899 exodus from Russia to Canada.

Directly or indirectly, Russian policy brought more than one utopian group to British Columbia at the turn of the century. Whereas the Sointulan Finns were basically secular socialists, the Doukhobors were radical Christians. The peasant sect resisted authority systematically, and they had a turbulent history in Russia. Breaking off from the Russian Orthodox Church in the eighteenth century, they were dubbed – by way of insult – *Dukhobortsi* ("spirit wrestlers") by the Archbishop Ambrosie of Ekaterinosla. By this, he meant "wrestlers against the Holy Spirit." But Doukhobor elders embraced the name, turning it to their advantage (much as homosexuals have done recently with the term 'queer'). "Strengthened by the spirit of Christ," they replied, "we wrestle against pride and fleshly lusts." They wrestled alongside, not against, the Holy Ghost. They were forced into exile after a dangerous confrontation with tsarist forces, known as the Burning of Arms, in 1894.

Doukhobor theology resembles Quaker and Anabaptist theology in some respects, rejecting above all the mediation of a priestly class. But it goes farther than either of these, rejecting the Bible as the ultimate source of authority.[2] The Doukhobors mistrust the written word, and rely instead on an evolving cycle of psalms and hymns, passed on orally, which is known as The Living Book of the Doukhobors. Dreams and visions are other sources of illumination. There are no Bibles, and no other outward trappings of religion in their meeting-halls, apart from a jug of water, a salt-cellar and a loaf of bread, which figure forth life's essentials.

The Doukhobor bows low in order to recognize the divine spark in fellow human beings. Utopianism shines through this key doctrinal point, from *Common Thoughts of the Christian Community of Universal Brotherhood*: "The world is based upon going forward; all things strive for perfection, and through this process seek to rejoin their source [God], as seeds yield ripe fruit." Just as a seed yields ripe fruit, so does humanity contain divine potential. The human being is the vessel of divine spirit, hence it is wrong to kill another person under any circumstances.

The group's leader, Peter "the Lordly" Verigin – referred to by his followers in the third person plural as "They" – affirmed Doukhobor pacifism and communalism in 1894 ("it is affirmed that the life of mankind is communal"), attracting the delighted attention of Count Leo Tolstoy, an anarcho-pacifist. The novelist denounced civilization, which had found its ultimate expression in capitalism's division of labour. He celebrated the virtues of hard physical work and the simple life. Born into the aristocracy, he had taken to wearing simple peasant blouses and making his own shoes. Some of his friends had tried to build utopias based on his ideas, but Tolstoy found them too self-conscious and over-intellectualized. He believed he had found his model society in the Doukhobors – pacifist agrarian communalists, living out this dream "naturally," without the promptings of education. Intellectuals like Matti Kurikka took inspiration from Tolstoy, while Tolstoy took sustenance from the spirit wrestlers.

The Doukhobors' exile was precipitated by the sect's pacifism, which lead Doukhobor men to refuse to serve in the tsar's army. In the 1894 protest known as the Burning of Arms, they turned out with their families to destroy, as a provocative flourish, all the guns, knives, and swords that came to hand. The authorities responded by beating the protesters, many of them nearly to death. Tolstoy himself intervened on the Doukhobors' behalf when the Tsar seemed poised to destroy them; in the end, Peter the Lordly and his followers were forced into exile.

The anarchist Peter Kropotkin, Tolstoy, and the American Quakers co-operated to help the Doukhobors escape. Kropotkin, who had himself been forced into exile on account of his anti-tsarist activism, chose the Canadian prairies for the peasants. A geographer by profession, he was drawn to the region because it resembled Russia. He negotiated with the Canadian government to ensure that the Doukhobors' principles would be respected. More than 7,000 Doukhobors made it to Saskatchewan as the century drew to a close. It was the largest single group to immigrate to Canada in this country's history.[3]

Officially, the Doukhobors were known as the Christian Community

The Doukhobor 'empire'
was built on fruit and jam
production.

of Universal Brotherhood. Living out their motto, "Toil and Peaceful Life," they cultivated land communally, but soon fell out with Saskatchewan authorities. In their 1986 book *The Doukhobors*, Ivan Akavumovic and George Woodcock (known to some as "Canada's Tolstoy" for his anarchist politics and support of Doukhobor causes), show how Doukhobor ideals automatically placed them at odds with the larger culture. Because they were pacifists, and a pledge of allegiance might lead to conscription (as it would in Russia), they refused to pledge allegiance to the King, and because they refused allegiance, they could not become citizens. Without becoming citizens, they could not hold title to their land. The Doukhobors replied that they didn't want to own the land in any case, but only to farm it. Because of this, and because land policy discouraged communal settlements, they ultimately lost over half the land they had cultivated. Most of them uprooted and resettled in British Columbia in 1909, lured by the pleasant weather west of the Rockies. This time, the land was registered, not communally, but in Peter Verigin's name. Verigin then willed the land to the community, anticipating that the mortage would be paid off in his lifetime.

For nearly thirty years, utopia flourished in the Kootenays, in the valleys that came to be known as "Consolation" and "Valley of Fruit." Largely self-sufficient, the community was "more successful than most North American communitarian experiments on a similarly ambitious scale," according to Avakumovic and Woodcock. The villages, vestigial today, were christened in a hopeful spirit. There was a whole constellation, forming a single community: Plodorodnoye ("Fruitful Glade"), Blagodatnoye ("Peace-giving"), Ostrow ("Island"), Prekrasnoye ("Most Beautiful"), Krestova ("Of the Cross"), and others. An abandoned gold-mining camp called Waterloo was settled and renamed Brilliant to erase the warlike association. All in all, Peter the Lordly acquired over 22,000 acres for producing fruit and fruit-products, lumber, and grain. Head-scarfed Russian peasants roamed the orchards, singing. Each village displayed the brick communal buildings, which, built along lines peculiar to the Doukhobors, housed virtually everyone. Two two-storey structures, each housing thirty-five people, were joined by a single-storey U-shaped building. Out back was a small barn and a steambath with separate sections for men and women. Each complex was surrounded by 100 acres of fields and orchards.

They were vegetarians, and ate together at long communal tables. They neither smoked nor drank. Every day they gathered for worship, seated on long benches, the men facing the women. Singing and chanting, they brought "the book" to life. But most of their time was devoted to cultivation. Until 1938, when the banks foreclosed on their mortgage and the Community assets were repossessed, they were fully self-supporting.

What brought the Doukhobor communities down seems to have been an unconscious alliance of internal and external forces. The Depression economy played a key role, of course. But it has been demonstrated that the government could probably have saved the Community if it had favoured communal enterprise in general, and the Doukhobors themselves in particular. The Doukhobors made outsiders uneasy. The situation worsened when Peter the Lordly was assassinated in 1924, together with eight of his companions, when their railway carriage was blown sky high as they travelled from Brilliant to Grand Forks. Though suspects abound, the murderers have never been identified. It is difficult to point the finger at the Sons of Freedom, for instance, since they felt no worse than ambivalent about the leader, and prided themselves on their pacifism, targeting only property in their drive against materialism. They in turn accuse nebulous government forces of trying to frame them. And the Russians have never been fully discounted.

The Doukhobor "crown" was passed to Peter the Lordly's son, Peter Petrovich, who came from Russia to his valley kingdom. The competing powers of the region, however, were growing uneasy. Woodcock and Avakumovic point to the way in which "makeshift" pioneer life, "which had room for large pockets of eccentricity, began to disappear as soon as land grew scarce and authority began to move in." Simultaneously, zealous Doukhobors started to react violently to the trappings of that authority, even as it bore down in earnest. Canadians of that era were not troubled by notions of multiculturalism. As urban imperatives grew to predominate over pioneer eccentricities, a great deal of pressure was exerted on the Doukhobors to hug the curves of bourgeois life. (This shift in B.C. culture is the central theme of Malcolm Lowry's novel *October Ferry to Gabriola*, in which Lowry becomes elegaic as the pastoral, anarchic, quasi-communal life of the squatters at Dollarton is squashed by urban encroachment. He contrasts the possibility of pioneer life with the new bureaucracy, symbolized by Vancouver. This drama was re-enacted in the 1960s and 1970s when hippies fled urban regulation. And it was these "latest agrarian rebels" who inspired renewed interest in the Doukhobors in the late 1960s.)

Repressiveness and zealotry fed off each other. The more outside authority manifested itself, the more zealous certain spirit wrestlers became; the more fanatical they appeared, the more the government interfered with them. There were three factions within the faith as a whole: Community Doukhobors (the "orthodox" group, which predominated), Independents (those who were inclined to assimilate with the larger society), and the radical Sons of Freedom, who attacked signs of assimilation and materialism wherever they perceived them. The main issues were registration – the Russians refused to register births, marriages, and deaths – and education. The Freedomites were not alone in using extremist tactics: police began exhuming Doukhobor bodies as part of their investigations. Large groups of people were jailed for failing to acknowldege births, marriages, and deaths — to signpost existence — in the accepted way. But this trouble was nothing compared to the battles which broke out over education.

IN THE 1890S, THE DISCOVERY OF SILVER brought a flood of fortune-seekers to the Kootenays. Dozens of mining towns were thrown up, virtually overnight. As the rush receded, some of these towns were abandoned, all but reabsorbed by the forest, which curled its way back in, winding round lamp-posts and garlanding fire hydrants. Some of them,

ТРУД И МИРНАЯ ЖИЗНЬ
ПЕТР ГОСПОДНІЙ.

TOIL AND PEACEFUL LIFE
PETER LORDLY (VERIGIN).

Doukhobor mourners at the funeral of their leader, Peter the Lordly, killed in a mysterious explosion in 1924.

the "drowned towns," were flooded by damming. Others, like New Denver, shrank to a manageable size and survived. New Denver, when it was founded by prospectors in 1890, was originally christened Eldorado (Argenta, a neighbouring town, later became home to a Quaker school and co-operative settlement).[4] One of its citizens, the wandering newspaperman Robert Thornton Lowery, remarked that "Paradise is the only rival to this little town." New Denver has played Paradise and Purgatory in turn to an alternating tide of outcasts, exiles and freedom seekers. About a decade after the Japanese were interned there, New Denver became the site of a draconian reform school for Freedomite children – draconian, not so much in its educational methods, but in the basis of its existence. Freedomite children were literally rounded up and incarcerated until school-leaving age.

The New Denver school was the ultimate expression of a more informal policy that had been going on for some years. The predominantly illiterate-and-proud-of-it Doukhobors viewed Canadian education as a tool of assimilation. In addition to regarding literacy as a kind of "fall" from authenticity in and of itself, they feared that state schools would promote an ideology which would lead straight to conscription. The authorities fined parents for keeping their children at home. The Sons of Freedom, in their turn, torched the schools. Nine schools were burned to the ground in 1923 alone. The government took the provocative measure of taking children away from their homes and locking them up in industrial schools. Their stated purpose was education, as well as "re-education": the children were to become average Canadians. The schools confirmed the Doukhobors' wildest fears, designed as they were to alienate the children from their way of life.

A 1932 newspaper article describes a visit to the girls' school, where the Freedomite daughters spun out their childhood years. The 100-or-so girls, aged seven to eighteen, were "a very motley crowd, garbed … in a kaleidoscopic array." The reporter finds the children oddly resistant. They "prefer to eat out of a common bowl, using their fingers." In this, they resembled the adults: Sons of Freedom protesters typically sat about naked on the floor, eating nuts and fruit with their fingers from a common pile.

After the Dominion government passed a law in 1931 making public nudity punishable by three years' incarceration, British Columbia's prisons began filling up with these dissident Doukhobors. The law in no way discouraged them, lured as they were by martyrdom. Nothing discouraged them – not even itching powder, which the police deployed on several occasions. Plans were laid to imprison them together on D'Arcy Island, a former leper colony in the Gulf Islands, just off Victoria. Ultimately, the penal colony was established on nearby Piers Island. There the Sons and Daughters of Freedom lived in separate quarters. In an ironic parody of Community life, they spent most of their time cultivating food for their own subsistence. The prison system was unprepared for vegetarian inmates.

Once released, many of these Sons and Daughters of Freedom made their way to Krestova, a rather arid and unsuccessful Community settlement, which was underpopulated and therefore welcomed newcomers. There, the Freedomites threw up their intentionally wretched little shacks, which they periodically burned to the ground in ritual gestures of renunciation. Naked and singing hymns, they would cast their clothes into the flames. From the 1920s to the 1960s, acts of Freedomite arson and dynamiting multiplied out of control. There were countless incidents throughout the Kootenays, involving Sons of Freedom, the other Doukhobors, and outsiders alike. No building was permanent, and you never knew what to expect. Many of the arsonists became addicted to fire-setting. One old lady known as "the firebug" was notorious for setting fires in court. Arraigned on arson charges, she would try to torch the courtroom furniture.

As a favour to Doukhobor leaders, Freedomite arsonists would occasionally burn their houses down as well: after all, why should a great man have to be bothered with such basic necessities? Assorted charismatic figures held sway at Krestova, such as Louis Popoff, "the Tsar of Heaven," who habitually wandered about in flowing white robes and a crown of oranges (Popoff was arrested in Nelson, arrayed, like the Emperor of yore, only in his orange-crown. He died in prison soon after). Another Freedomite leader, Michael "the Archangel" Verigin, led a group of followers to found a millenial commune at Gilpin, near Qualicum Beach on Vancouver Island, a location which had been revealed to him in a dream. There they lived well into the 1950s in a cluster of cedar cabins, surrounded by neat gardens, awaiting the Second Coming. Gilpin was to be the site of the New Jerusalem. In an unconscious echo of Brother Twelve, the Archangel designated his followers as ushers-in of the post-apocalypse. The Gilpin residents were visited in 1954, not by heavenly deputies, but by the police, who had come to collect Doukhobor children for the school at New Denver.

The children had never been to school. Woodcock describes a pathetic scene of terrified children, running to hide in the woods around Gilpin. Krestova was raided as well. Krestova villagers followed en masse, and camped around the gates of the New Denver School, crying and chanting from the Living Book. Outside, the grieving group of nude parents. Inside, the stunned and disoriented children, involuntary students, mostly illiterate. How well did they speak English, one wonders, these Freedomite kids? Ranged by day in rows of inkwelled desks, by night they drowsed in rows of single beds. They were snatched up and locked up with Dickensian severity, but at least they had each other. No-one jeered at their nude parents, because there were no students but themselves. No-one sneered, except, perhaps, their teachers. But these were pretty fair, by all reports.

In its six years of existence, about 170 children passed through the New Denver school, which produced both scholars and firebombers, a new generation. The school closed in 1960, releasing its mistreated young into a growing stream of liberation theologists, a new wave of protest which crossed ethnic lines and histories, a more generalized kind of No.

All in all, although the threads of tradition are traceable, and the Sons of Freedom still light up the pages of the *Province* newspaper from time to time, among the Doukhobors in general the trend has been assimilationist. Some persisted in the old ways, but many more got regular jobs, or went to university. And at university, as the sixties turned into "The Sixties," some got into peace and vegetarianism and protest and nudism with a whole new constellation of meanings interwoven. Now, nudity, instead of announcing "I am a Doukhobor, here is our story and our demands," would announce a whole other agenda: the virtues of sex, sexual innocence, and childlike freedom. The end of world history and the dawning of a new era. Did another spirit hover still behind the bulk of those new nudists, a wispy utopian ghost behind that heavy utopian body, the fading spirit of a wrestler?

Rival Worlds

It's about a commune of cannibals living off a commune of vegetarians
in the north of B.C.

> – Susan Musgrave, describing her 1980 novel
> *The Charcoal Burners*

MUCH OF THE ACTIVITY WE THINK OF AS "The Sixties" in fact took
place in the 1970s. The back-to-the-land movement is a case in point.
Certainly, the movement was inspired by the 1960s, and arguably
inspired by the failure of the 1960s. The student revolutions of 1968 led,
not to heaven on earth, but to the dreary, bludgeoning brutality of
places like Altamont, the rock festival that went horribly wrong. In the
early sequences of the film *Gimme Shelter*, a glib Mick Jagger speaks of
rock festivals as a "microcosm" of the good society that was to unfold
imminently. But after that emblematic day, nasty, brutish, and immea-
surably long, when the hippies revealed their seamy innards, only two
retreats seemed possible. One was the cocaine-bright nights of discothe-
ques like Studio 54. The other was the backwoods of North America. As
the 1970s dawned, hipsters all over the continent shook off their hang-

*In the summertime, the
commune dwellers felt closer
to their ideal: the tribe.*

overs and waded into the bush, pursued by cries of "Escapists!" and "Cop-out!" from the stranded urban revolutionaries left behind. British Columbia was a prime destination.

"Looking for land in B.C. ... ," Mark Vonnegut wrote of that period, "just about everyone wanted to stay long into the night talking about that one."[1] Ken Lester, who under the pseudonym "Alice" wrote a practical column on intentional communities called "Tribes" for the then-radical *Georgia Straight*, recalls the bundles of letters he received from people enquiring about free land in British Columbia. In the public imagination, B.C. was "the end of the line," the last frontier, the last place on earth.

Within a few years, the province was stuffed with communes. Every dirt road and every trail in the forest seemed to lead to a motley group of cabins, a geodesic dome or an old converted schoolbus with chickens scratching on the roof and a clump of dope-smoking longhairs nodding within. As miniature nations, they gave themselves names, such as Kosmunity, Centre of the World Beautiful, Bar None Farm, Locus, Harmony Farmstead Co-op, the Space Feather Family, Workshare Farm, Earth Seed, and Pepperland.

Ensconced in their woodsy communes, they found their hands full. There were chores to be done. There were chickens to be fed, kerosene lamps to be cleaned, outhouses to be built, zucchini to be pickled, or made into bread, or otherwise got rid of. But the charge of escapism still stung. The issue came up over and over at the regular meetings of the British Columbia Coalition of Intentional Co-operative Communities (CICC), self-described as "an amorphous network of groups and individuals," and in its newsletter, *Open Circle*. One commune dweller, an American in self-imposed exile who called himself Mason Dixon, scoffed at the rankling charges, insisting that there was no escape from the corporate establishment, what with B.C. Hydro and MacMillan Bloedel camped at the gates of utopia. The backwoods of B.C. were as much the front lines as anywhere else on earth. This is not what he or his friends had expected.

Terry Simmons, who wrote a 1979 thesis on B.C. back-to-the-landers, describes the movement as "an optimistic response to an essentially pessimistic view of life," namely, an apocalyptic one.[2] A basic belief in the inevitability of widespread ecological disaster, to say nothing of nuclear holocaust, formed the backdrop for this move to the country. Mark Vonnegut, whose book *The Eden Express* documents a communal experiment near Powell River (and his subsequent slide into schizophrenia, paralleling disenchantment), is eloquent on this subject: "A fair amount of our lives was tied to hypothetical situations – the revolution, ecological disaster, the last judgement, the breakdown of Western civilization, Armageddon."

To CICC members, these spectres were practically tangible. Then as now, it was difficult to tease apart fact from cultural hallucination – the evident decay of the environment, and the accompanying sense of doom, from the lateness of the millenium; the fact of war from the threat of war. These concerns united the disparate communes under the amorphous roof of the CICC.

In the mid-1970s, the CICC's network involved more than 100 member groups. Each issue of the coalition newsletter was produced by a different member community, which would include a self-profile. And every few months, a different group would host the CICC conference. One host group, the Quakers of the Kootenay Co-operative Land Settlement Society, could trace its pastoral return back to the 1950s, when several Quaker families came north "searching for a life of simplicity in harmony with nature."[3] They came north from California in a caravan of Model As and settled in Argenta, an old silver-mining town, in 1952 (it is likely that their connection to the Doukhobors brought the Kootenays to their attention). They quickly formed the Argenta Monthly Meeting of Friends, and built a meeting house in 1954. In 1959 they founded the Argenta Friends School,[4] a secondary school, and the Argenta Friends Press, which publishes *Canadian Friend* and other Quaker texts. This was the context, then, for the founding of the land co-operative, on 230 acres near Kootenay Lake, in 1971. The co-op (and most other such land co-ops, as opposed to communes) aims at a balance of individualism and communalism. House sites are owned by individual families, and the remainder of the land is common land. In true Quaker fashion, which overlaps with anarchism, the co-op strives for a spirit of consensus.

The CICC member communities were not exclusively rural. Jim Bowman, a young archivist who did a lot of work with the Coalition, represented the New Westminster Co-op, a communal house in downtown New Westminster, founded in 1967 by a scattering of radicals from Simon Fraser University.[5] Another academic dream produced the Alternate Community, which grew out of a Vancouver Free University class on intentional communities, actual and imagined. In fact, the Alternate Community might be symbolized by a small library – the course-books which engendered and constituted it. In 1974, when the Free U folded, the Alternate Community discussion group, still in the planning stages, inherited this library as a contribution towards the future commune. Their promotional newsletter, which came out of a house on West 13th Avenue in Vancouver, and was designed to stir up interest in the idea, was sprinkled with quotes from the library's books, such as Benjamin Zablocki's *The Joyful Community*, Murray Bookchin's *Post-Scarcity Anarchism*, and Germaine Greer's *The Female Eunuch*. The document ends with a quote from Robert Theobald's *Modern Utopian*: "Social change happens because somebody makes it happen. The great disadvantage of (written) history is that it makes history (what actually took place) look inevitable."

The Alternate Community newsletter, in anticipation of an actual community, is a history of what might happen, a history of possibilities, and in this it becomes a kind of literary utopia. Other CICC members, in varying stages of development, offered other utopian manuscripts, sometimes in the pages of *Open Circle* (promoting fantasy was one of its primary purposes). Some were paper utopias, while others had a certain material reality, but needed help reaching their assorted goals (full communalism, non-sexism, a credit system, or whatever). Their advertisements took on the tone, and, in retrospect, the pathos, of an ad in the personals.

The Fantasy Farm of Enderby, B.C., was situated on 160 acres with lakes, rivers, and mountains nearby. "Presently we raise alfalfa and beef cows … We are an intentional community working towards being non-competitive, equalizing work and diminishing traditional roles (sex, position, etc.) … Our present goals are to fix up the house, add a bathroom (the foundation is already laid!), repair the barn, and for the farm to become more self-sufficient. We would like to have more children here with a school and separate living quarters for them. We're interested in living with a variety of people (as to age, race, interest and beliefs) …"[6]

The Nelson Group, a "community aware and interested in the events of the world – and thankful for having its distance from the greater part of the holocaust," offered alongside its list of community assets ("a ski doo … a broken 1962 VW bug and van … a potting wheel …") a section entitled Three Fantasies. These contributions to the history of possibilities nearly constitute a separate counterculture literary genre in and of themselves. They are superlatively earnest and hopeful to the point of heartbreak. They represent deeply felt dreams, and as such they somehow make one cringe a little, these wish lists: "There will be deep, repression-free relationships amongst each other … There will be a hermitage hut where people can draw away from worldly activity and be supported by the community while they explore their inner natures … Things that might happen: … raising bees … running 'schools of living,' teaching homestead skills, farming, yoga, encounter and nature lore … "

ONE CICC MEMBER GROUP HAD NO PATIENCE with such airy imaginings. For them, there were two kinds of communes – spiritual and revolutionary — and spirituality had no place on a revolutionary commune. When they hosted the coalition conference in 1977, a sign posted at the beginning of the four-mile muddy trail into their land read: "This way to the revolution." Still thriving today near 100 Mile House, they are known as CEEDS (Community Education and Economic Development Society). But in the mid-seventies they seemed to change their name every few months, from the Ochiltree Organic Commune to the Cariboo Organic Commune to the Troopers Commune, and so on, in tandem with their ideological shifts. Disgusted with the namby-pamby nature of *Open Circle*, the Marxist-Leninist CEEDS collective denounced the CICC, splintered off, and began issuing their own crudely illustrated mimeographed newsletter, *In Defense of Nature*, which chronicled the commune's history and ongoing adventures. *In Defense of Nature* also chronicles the group's rigorous policy of self-criticism, with unintentionally comical results. By the mid-seventies, the hippie movement had become awfully tepid, and it rankled the fiery folk of CEEDS. "Where have all the hippies gone?" was their constant lament. Disillusion was creeping in. As someone noted in *Open Circle*, "the number of people living in community in B.C. as for the rest of North America seems to be declining."

CEEDS dug their heels in. Using a reading list of Jim Bowman's, they organized a theory group that met regularly for awhile in a nearby field. The end product was their own little red book, *The Revolutionary Hippy Manifesto*. But CEEDS has always been controversial, and not just among the "straights." As a German correspondent named Wolfgang wrote them, "I've observed that people in B.C. communities make strange faces and show uneasy feeling when they talk about your commune." Today CEEDS is widely respected in the community, in particular for their organic farming projects. People come from around the world to study their techniques. They have arrived at a solid place — but they chose a rocky road in.

CEEDS founders Jerry and Nancy LeBourdais came to the Cariboo in 1971 and soon began squatting on Crown land at Borland meadow, near Williams Lake. Instead of living in peaceful isolation, they were immensely confrontational. They soon fell out with a lot of the residents

CEEDS founder Jerry LeBourdais, wearing his ever-present Mao hat, harvesting vegetables in one of the commune's gardens, around 1992.

in the area. The turbulent history of CEEDS, punctuated by active protests, court appearances, and occasional gunfire, reads like one long answer to charges of escapism. The commune was nothing if not politically engaged.

CEEDS' activities revolved around a complicated alliance with the native street people of Williams Lake, known as the Troopers. The Troopers, a loose community made up of mostly Carrier, Chilcotin, and Shuswap Indians, were a thorn in the side of the better-dressed citizenry of Williams Lake. Neither were they particularly popular with the local Sugar Cane Indian band. They were mostly alcoholics, and hung around the local liquor store drinking and panhandling. They were homeless. Every winter, it seemed, someone from among their ranks froze to death. Nobody wanted to know. Everyone wished they would just disappear, except a bunch of crazed commie pot-smoking free-love hippies from the bush, who held them in a peculiar kind of reverence. The raggedy Troopers, poor and despised, were an embarrassment to "straight" society, and the hippies loved them for it. They felt that the Troopers had something to offer them.

At Metlakatla and Meanskinish, European society was presented as a model for native people, but what is perhaps more significant for the history of utopias is the way in which the imagined life of native people has been a model for Europeans. This is particularly true of hippie communes (hence the *Georgia Straight*'s "Tribes" column). Someone writes in *In Defense of Nature* of "the knowledge to be gained through living with the Indian people," which may be true enough, but as a sentiment, it is common in counterculture circles. CEEDS differed from other hippies in that they didn't merely idealize native culture, but actually tried to merge with it, in their own unique way, and their attempts were put on display in the summer of 1979 at the Williams Lake Stampede Parade.

A mortified hush fell over the crowd. An alarming spectacle had drawn into view. A renegade float. Who the hell gave permission for this? High atop a decorated truck sat a motley band of Troopers and hippies, nodding and waving triumphantly. Some played drums and chanted, while others smoked a peace pipe. One of them rhythmically dipped a salmon net over the edge of the pickup. Produce lay about, suggesting abundance. The truck was festooned with posters, emblazoned with images of peace pipes and wine jugs marked XXX. They read, in handpainted letters: TROOPERS ARE HIGH.

The original site of contact was a community garden on the Sugar Cane Reserve. The commune first planted the garden around 1976 and invited the Troopers to a work party. That way, both groups could feed themselves. The hippies could fulfill the utopian dream of self-sufficiency, and the Troopers would no longer have to rely on handouts. The hippies were excited, bristling with hope and energy. Everyone was to arrive bright and early. There would be no booze. That was their first mistake. Only one or two Troopers showed up.

Taken aback, the commune dwellers called for a round of rigorous self-criticism, and emerged with a new policy. They had been wrong, they decided, typically bourgeois in their hangups. They had blindly imposed their preconceived notions about sobriety on the Troopers. Who did they think they were? "Alcohol is not a problem," they concluded. "It is only white society that perceives it as such." Prohibition was lifted in the garden, and the next work party was a great success. The garden flourished, generating ideas as well as zucchini: "As you walk in the moonlight to the brow of the hill, you can see people sitting around the campfire discussing revolution." It was the first of many such projects. CEEDS' five organic farms are still going strong today.

The commune moved from hesitant acceptance of drinking to downright anti-sobriety. Drunkenness was defiance, a slap in the face of the bourgeoisie. It was messy and fabulous. And the frequent references to "sharing the wine" with the Troopers in *In Defense of Nature* suggest a meaning-saturated act, a kind of communion. They joined in with a vengeance, chasing Calona Red (they abolished wine snobbery) with vanilla extract: "We share the vanilla extract … it's a good drink." The hippies, who had begun calling themselves the Troopers Commune to

CEEDS members with some of the commune's horses, around 1992. Once Williams Lake's worst nightmare, CEEDS is now widely respected in the community for their organic farming techniques.

make themselves indistinguishable from their street brothers, now began supplying vanilla extract at cut-rate prices from their new co-op store. The store, also sited on the Sugar Cane Reserve, was associated with Vancouver's Fed-up Food Co-op.

Here, too, they had to learn a lesson in humility. The initial plan was to introduce the Troopers and the band to healthy whole-grain eating: brown rice, whole wheat flour, molasses and such. But nobody came, and all their good intentions moldered on the shelves alongside the rolled oats. It was the community garden story all over again.

A meeting was held. It was resolved: they had made the same annoying mistake! Typical crypto-bourgeois patronizing attitudes. Once again, they had tried to inflict their "whiteman headspace" on the natives, who were having none of it. The people had spoken, writes the *In Defense of Nature* journalist. "From listening to the people" (their eloquent silence) "we have found that they are the ones that know their needs. For instance, the people want white rice, white sugar, white flour, and pop and candy." So they began stocking these forbidden goodies. Another thing the people wanted was meat, which the commune began supplying in great quantities, raising free-range chickens and pigs.

It is remarkable how politicized food became in the counterculture. CEEDS was (and is) virulently anti-vegetarian. Anti-vegetarianism was a stick to beat the other hippie communes with, a way of distinguishing themselves from these others. Vegetarianism was flakey New Age mysticism. Not a few CICC meetings were rocked by this issue (most of the other member groups wouldn't touch meat). CEEDS saw organic farming, and not vegetarianism, as the alternative to the evils of mass-production livestock. Organic farming came under the banner of liberation ("Free the Pigs and let them Root!"), as did their practice, picked up from the street folk, of scavenging the garbage from behind the local Super-Valu and feeding it to their animals ("We urge others to go ahead and liberate this 'garbage'"). CEEDS' new, revolutionized relationship with animals began when they freed twenty leghorn pullets from Pacific Hatcheries in Vancouver. The CEEDS chickens and pigs wandered freely among the communards, even taking part in a revolutionary play entitled "Good – But Not Easy."

Like so many of their contemporaries, the CEEDS members were relentless in their pursuit of the "natural." Vegetarianism, anti-vegetarianism: both were roads to Nature, or so hoped the travellers. Nature, that vast, elusive subject, presented an ever-receding horizon to the hippie movement. All of their practice was pointed at it, but nobody could agree on the nature of the natural. Eating was to be natural, as was sex, though this presented endless complications. People denied their undeniable feelings, all in the name of the natural. Jealousy, for example, was banished from utopia. The official word on the CEEDS commune was: "Monogamous couples and the accompanying head-space have no place on a revolutionary commune … Certainly the resulting feelings of jealousy are not a natural thing in humans." The writer allows a hint of uncertainty to creep into this pronouncement, noting that humans "are descended from apes and it is unsure whether they are monogamous."

Pending the definitive word on apes, then, monogamy was suspended.

MEANWHILE, AT NEARBY 100 MILE HOUSE, a rival Cariboo realm was thriving. Hierarchical, even monarchical, highly New Age, superlatively nice and displaying a bland middlebrow aesthetic, the Emissaries of Divine Light present a neat antithesis to CEEDS. Whereas the Marxists were confrontational, the Emissaries were courtly and conciliatory. CEEDS members literally strove for crudeness (one wrote of the need to unlearn a polished writing style), while the Emissaries embraced refinement. The Emissaries were not hippies. The organization, like the Brother Twelve's Aquarian Foundation, has its roots between the world wars. Like CEEDS, the Emissaries still exist today, though in a diminished state. Since the death of their adored leader, Lord Martin Cecil, later Exeter, in 1988, the Emissaries have undergone some profound changes.

Martin, as he is generally known, became infatuated with the Cariboo at age twenty-one and lived there most of his life, following in the tradition of another recurrent British Columbian cultural pattern, that of the remittance man. He was one of the province's most distinguished remittance men, as well as one of its most prominent utopians. Martin was that rare thing, a truly beautiful man. To a certain extent, the Emissaries can be understood as a cult of the beautiful man. The Emissaries had their start with Lloyd Meeker, a.k.a. Uranda, an American visionary, but it took a partnership with Martin to really get them off the ground. Martin's admirers always insist upon his physical and spiritual beauty, which combined to form a beacon, a paragon; to join forces with this paragon was intensely flattering. It was recognition of the kind people wait for all their lives. Martin personified an invitation to spiritual aristocracy. It was as though his earthly position corresponded to some sort of transcendent excellence, and all of the Emissaries wanted a part of it. He was charismatic but not sinister, producing a quiet, seemly rapture in his followers. "The first time I heard him speak," recalls one woman admirer, "it was heaven."[7]

Martin Cecil was born in 1909 and raised in patrician splendour at Burghley House, built by his ancestor William Cecil during the reign of Elizabeth I. His official biographer, Chris Foster, draws many parallels between Martin and this earlier Cecil, who was Elizabeth's Lord High Treasurer and close adviser. She made him the first Lord Burghley (a later Cecil received the title Marquess of Exeter). For Foster, Martin's life virtually began at his confirmation into the Church of England, which was apparently a great disappointment to him. Hoping for an epiphany and feeling nothing, young Martin felt a kind of spiritual deficit which eventually led him to the crown of the Emissaries. As a second son, he was expected to go into the army, the navy, or the church. After a stint in the navy, during which he met his glamorous future wife, a high-strung Hungarian with darkly shadowed eyes, Martin travelled to British Columbia to take charge of his father's ranch.

In 1930, British Columbia was a place where anything could happen. Brother Twelve knew this. On De Courcy Island, his fantasy kingdom was in full flower. Martin Cecil was no Brother Twelve, being neither mad, bad, nor dangerous to know. But like the Brother, he was attracted and inspired by the no-place quality of the province. At 100 Mile House, where Martin had the run of 15,000 acres, possibilities unrolled infinitely. Foster remarks that in England, "the physical pioneering had been done long ago, while 100 Mile House was virtually a blank; there was nothing there. Whatever happened would be entirely up to him." In William Cecil's era, all of America had seemed like that. But by 1930, civilized life had painted itself into a corner, and British Columbia had inherited the last-frontier mantle. As one of the last "empty" places in North America, it attracted its share of adventurers. Every so often, one of these lone figures would loom up on the landscape.

One of these was Conrad O'Brien-ffrench, whose adventures during World War I and later in pre-war Nazi Germany made him the model for Ian Fleming's 007 character. He befriended Martin, and together they fell under the spell of Lloyd Meeker, or Uranda. O'Brien-ffrench and Martin were drawn to this sort of thing. They had read up on Rosicrucianism, and now they were intrigued by Uranda. Perhaps it is fortunate they never met Brother Twelve. O'Brien-ffrench and Martin were wealthy, well-bred, and hungry for answers, and they would have been ideal targets for him. Like Brother Twelve's Aquarian Foundation, Uranda's Emissaries of Divine Light were born out of the unease of the period between the wars, with its Great Depression and political turbulence.

New Age philosophies represent the bright side of the apocalypse. The New Age is an apocalypse (from the Greek word meaning "unveiling") of optimism – the present order will give way all at once to a better order – and in this it effects a retrieval of the Christian notion of apocalypse. Our equation of apocalypse with absolute end (the Bomb) is secular in origin – much of contemporary life has been haunted by a strong belief in the imminence of nuclear holocaust. For pre-modernism, the apocalypse, for all its violence, nonetheless ushered in the reign of heaven on earth. And this is more or less what New Age philosophies anticipate. The Aquarians and the Emissaries thus had common

An unlikely twosome: English blueblood Lord Martin Exeter and poor-boy American Uranda, 1940s.

The Lodge, centre of Emissary life, was built by Martin Exeter in the 1930s to replace the original 100 Mile House, which had burned down.

roots, but played themselves out differently. Like the Aquarians, the Emissaries had a sense of mission. They were chosen. Brother Twelve was a messenger from the Aquarians. And the Emissaries, as their name suggests, were messengers too. They had their own sense of purpose on earth – to invite humanity spiritwards.

Plain old Lloyd Meeker, a poor boy from Iowa, son of a circuit minister, was visited by divine light. For three days solid he scribbled revelations in his lonely room, and emerged as Uranda. Following in his father's footsteps, he hit the road, a travelling mystical healer among others. His philosophy of spiritual realignment bore a strange relationship to chiropractic, and indeed there were a number of chiropractors among his devotees. Uranda understood the Fall in terms of a spiritual misalignment which accounted for all our miseries. Like a distorted spinal cord, humanity was out of line with spirit. Uranda's program of "attunement," designed to heal this rift, amounted to spiritual chiropractic. It was a hands-off approach, however. He would not touch his patients, but hold his hands over their chakras and meditate.

He is seen by the Emissaries as a teacher on par with Jesus. Or perhaps, more accurately, he plays John the Baptist to Martin's Jesus. Foster shamelessly compares Martin to Jesus throughout his biography, simultaneously elevating Martin and bringing Jesus down to a merely human level: "Jesus, we are told, sensed at the age of twelve the shallowness of the usual human goals, and the fact of a transcendent purpose in life … A traumatic moment in Martin's own awakening came at the age of fifteen when he was confirmed in the Church of England." Martin is also compared to the Buddha and to Arjuna of Hinduism. In their homogenization of world religions, the Emissaries resemble the Unitarians. They de-emphasize Christ's divinity, preferring to see him as an especially enlightened individual. Jesus was one, and Martin was another one: "Many times over the ages an individual has emerged on the planet and brought inspiration, a light, to others."

Martin and Uranda found that light in each other when they met in Vancouver in 1940. That same year saw the beginning of the Lodge community at 100 Mile House, in the hostelry Martin had built to replace the old House, the original gold-rush rest-stop. At first the community was small – ten or so members. Its sister "unit" was Uranda's ranch at Loveland, Colorado. When Uranda's plane crashed in California in 1954, killing him and several other Emissaries, Martin became the leader of the group, giving regular "art of living" courses as Uranda had done, and corresponding with a network of people around the world. Eventually this network crystallized into ten new communities, bringing the total number to twelve. There were units in England and France. There was even a unit in South Africa.

The Emissaries' expansion was bolstered by a dynastic marriage between Martin's son, Michael, and Uranda's daughter, Nancy Rose, in 1967. The Emissaries were great respecters of marriage and of appointed sex roles in general. Well into the 1970s, there were distinct "patterns" (a "pattern" is the Emissary term for a particular activity, or organizing principle) for men and women. Men farmed, for example, while women baked. Nearby in Williams Lake, CEEDS wrestled with monogamy and other "sexisms." But in the Lodge community at 100 Mile House, only married couples were permitted to live together. They were careful to avoid any hint of the kind of sexual scandal that plagues intentional communities.

The Emissaries of today offer different reasons to account for the upheaval which plagues them. Some members feel that patriarchal patterns undermined the Emissaries from within, that the hierarchy failed to "hear the female voice," that it was thus too weak to bear the death of the leader. The female voice of the Emissaries is personified in Nancy Rose Meeker, who recently became separated from Michael. (It seems that, like the title Marquess of Exeter, the role of leader is hereditary. But just as Michael became leader, his marriage dissolved.) Nancy Rose, every inch her father's daughter, is a visionary in her own right, boiling with fancies and speaking with spirits. She writes mystical texts of her own and travels about, speaking at the remaining units. At Edenvale, a pastoral compound in the Fraser Valley, Nancy Rose facilitates a woman's retreat called "Listening to the Inner Voice."

The future of the Emissaries is uncertain. Some of them, in a true millenial spirit, see the Emissary breakdown as a symptom of worldwide chaos. Martin has not been reborn in Michael, the present leader. Michael inherited his father's title and his aquiline beauty, but not his intense sense of mission. From behind his bright blue eyes shines a more ordinary soul – sweet, even radiant, but ordinary nonetheless. Divine ecstasies are not his department. The Emissaries are in a state of flux, having to reduce kingdoms of spirit to mere businesses – organic farms, conference centres – and their numbers are depleted. But as the turn of the century draws on apace, who knows what might emerge from these calm, mannerly folk? Somewhere in the mists of Vancouver slumbers Michael and Nancy's son Anthony, a young man with a magical genetic makeup. Uranda's grandson, William Cecil's descendant, he is heir to the Exeter title and heir apparent of the Emissaries. Who knows, in the unrevealed tomorrow of British Columbia, what kind of new utopian king might awake?

Lowry's Legacy

The hitchhikers have heard it is still possible to live down on the beach ...

– Jack Hodgins, *Spit Delaney's Island*

MALCOLM LOWRY MAY BE DEAD, but his presence is still felt in the bar-rooms of Vancouver. He is the patron saint of the three-week bender. Bookish boys still stagger from bar to bar, clutching dog-eared copies of *Under the Volcano* and roaring about dipsomania. They trace a wavy line down Hastings Street all the way to Burnaby, where they order chasers at the Malcolm Lowry Room. Next stop on the literary tour is the site of Lowry's poor little shack on the beach at Dollarton. Across from the fuming Shell Oil plant which Lowry hated, and which to him stood for everything awful – famously, the 'S' in the neon sign had burned out, adding insult to injury – gulls wheel and the salt water laps at the shore. This place was Paradise, and the Shell Oil plant its antithesis. British Columbia, cool and blue, is longed for as a kind of heaven in the dusty Mexican underworld of *Volcano*. In *October Ferry to Gabriola*, Dollarton is Edenic in the extreme, brimming over with wild creatures:

A Mudflats home, circa 1970.
Houses were built on piles,
which kept them out of the
water at high tide.

Behind the cabin, which had been sold to them lock, stock and barrel for $100, were forty acres of forest to wander in: sometimes at night curious raccoons came right into the house, and in spring, through the casement windows, they watched the deer swimming across the water ... [1]

It was here that Lowry squatted in style with his wife, Marjorie, who played Eve to his boozy Adam, in a small community of stilted squats that lined the water's edge. The Lowrys lived there from 1939 to 1954. "A successful novelist ... is 'king' of the beach squatters," wrote a journalist in 1947. "The Lowrys ... have watched a squatter town grow up around them." At the time, at the margins of Vancouver, there were a few squatter communities, "Vancouver's human driftwood," in Coal Harbour, False Creek, and Stanley Park. Considering how hard North Vancouver's civic government tried to rid itself of them, the Dollarton squatters were pretty tenacious. They managed to hang on until 1957, when the colony was finally bulldozed. Perhaps the very last to go were the nearby Mudflats dwellers, in the early 1970s. Caught between worlds, clinging to stilt-houses in the disputed territory below the high-tide mark, the crablike squatters constituted a form of intertidal life.

Lowry's *mode de vie*, living cheaply off the superabundance of the coastal environment, has long been a model for local artists. His Dollarton life was Edenic rather than utopian per se, though a kind of community did grow up among the squatters there. Lowry is dead, but many of the writers who met him were still around in 1995. Al Purdy, for instance, or Al Neil, who has had a Deep Cove shack of his own since 1966. The 1960s squatter community at the Mudflats, which housed quite a few artists and intellectuals, carried on the Lowry tradition. The sculptor Tom Burrows lived there, as did Dr. Paul Spong, the University of B.C. psychiatrist and well-known killer whale researcher.

Places like the Mudflats colony were possessed of a lucky spirit, the spirit of fortuitous order, which springs up unplanned and unregulated. Things just seem to work out. The Mudflats shacks were salvaged shacks, made of driftwood, that ubiquitous B.C. stuff, and other found materials. "It's impossible to live here and not get cooled out," Spong said of his beloved village, which came under threat of demolition around 1970.[2] An idea was floated to move the whole colony to Bralorne, an abandoned mining town northwest of Lillooet, as part of a larger plan to start a utopian community there. A lot of bohemians were set to buy shares in the venture. This never came to pass, though Bralorne has been the site of many an idealistic fantasy. Like a sort of Ghost of Future Past, it keeps reappearing in the history of B.C. utopias, conjuring up what might have been (Bralorne is currently inhabited by an evangelical Christian group).

B.C. ARTISTS' COMMUNITIES HAVE AIMED at a perfect balance between individualism and communalism. The Western Front, an urban arts collective, was founded in the early 1970s, even as the bulldozers loomed at the edges of the Mudflats. Collectivism was in the air, but so was a burgeoning unease with rigid politics and hippie earnestness. Where the hippies were serious and faux-rustic, the Western Front crowd was playful, glamorous, and urban. In a way, they melded collectivism and 1970s Studio 54 decadence. "The Front" has always embraced absurdism. The building, a dark old wood-panelled place, is strewn with vestiges of its former occupants, the Knights of Pythias, a fraternal society founded in the nineteenth century. A helmeted emblem hangs in the second-floor washroom, and in other odd spots around the building. When the artists moved in, they discovered a lot of old ceremonial props – spears, fans, coffins, and other things that came in handy for performances. Theatricality was the order of the day. The Western Front has always cultivated performance, conceptual, and multimedia art, rather intimate work that lends itself well to notions of community. There was a happy mix of idealism and practicality. Video art, a Western Front specialty, required expensive equipment, and this is where the arts collective came in. With help from the nurturing climate of the Trudeau-era

An "auto-portrait" by early
members of the Western
Front, 1973.

Canada Council, which showered money down upon the arts, they
could buy the right machinery and share it among themselves. They
helped with each other's "pieces," they sat in each other's audiences,
they lived together, ate together, and hobnobbed together. As they had
hoped, art bled into life, so that the two became indistinguishable.

Most members had pseudonyms, and soon their pseudonyms were
interchangeable with their real names. Eric Metcalfe and his then-wife
Kate Craig were Doctor and Lady Brute. With their signature leopard-
skin outfits, they inhabited Metcalfe's alternate world, Brutopia. Glenn
Lewis was known as Flakey Rosehips. He was involved in, among other
things, water ballet performance art. Vincent Trasov, in the guise of Mr.
Peanut, ran for Mayor of Vancouver in 1974, and won 3.6 per cent of the
popular vote.

Western Front members soon began colonizing the nearby Sunshine
Coast, establishing land co-ops at Roberts Creek and Storm Bay, past
the end of Highway 101. The rainy Sunshine Coast, dubbed with the

tourist trade in mind, was growing famous for the network of communes to be found there, among them the Eagle's Nest, the Bayview Project, the Legal Front, the General Store, the Funny Food Farm, and the Crowe Road Farm, which still exists today. Mark Vonnegut chronicled his Sunshine Coast commune memories and schizophrenia attack in *The Eden Express*, while Paul Williams chronicled his in *Apple Bay, or Life on the Planet*. It was hippie heaven up in the bush, but down in the towns, it was hell. The "straights" declared war on the invaders, banning hitchhikers from the highway and longhairs from the restaurants. Signs were posted: No Hippies. The *Peninsula Times* called them "deadbeats" and "undesirables" and wondered "how many American draft dodgers swell the ranks."[3]

People flocked to the Sunshine Coast because the living was easy there. It was countryside, but pretty close to Vancouver by ferry. It was wild yet civilized, miles of evergreen and alder forest punctuated by well-stocked, well-serviced towns. It was rainy and grey through the winter and into April, but seldom cold. With a little grant money, you could start a small farm. Sometimes, especially in August, as you roamed from bush to bush picking blackberries, it seemed you could live easily off the land. Salmonberries were plentiful, as were salal and huckleberries. There was a lot of salvageable wood, to say nothing of trees, and the creeks were bursting with fish. It was truly "the land where Nature gave you a little help," as Jack Hodgins describes coastal B.C.

A number of artists began dividing their time between Vancouver and the Sunshine Coast. Babyland, so called after one particularly fertile summer, lies hidden from sight in the Roberts Creek woods. You had to approach Babyland on foot – park at the end of Raspberry Road and trudge through the trees along the creek. It was a green and sparkling scene, with emerald-coloured feathery lace ferns scattered about, and stones covered with deep moss. Now and then you came across a colossal burned-out stump, vestige of the old-growth forest, with salal sticking out of it like a shock of coarse hair. There in the midst of sword ferns was a lone enamel bathtub, pillaged from some demolition site, its lion paws planted in ashes. On warm days someone would fill it with creek water, light a fire beneath it and bathe in the sun. There were three cedar houses laid out in a rough triangle. One belonged to Mick Henry, a potter in the heavy brown style of the day. One belonged to Mr. Peanut, who participated in the Image Bank's "colour bar" project: colour bars, rectangular blocks striped with all the shades of the rainbow, were stacked around his house and all over the common land. The third house belonged to Carole Itter and her small yellow-haired daughter, Lara. Carole, a visual and performance artist, was obsessed with chickens. She was sewing a frying-egg costume for her new piece, soon to be debuted at the Front. Clad in her gauzy whites and yellows, she would lie on the floor, vibrating and jumping as she fried in an imaginary frying pan.

For the artists, as for a lot of British Columbians, there are graduating levels of isolation. Vancouverites may retreat to Roberts Creek, while Roberts Creekers go to Storm Bay. And sometimes Roberts Creek simply isn't remote enough for urban fantasists. You can't drive to Storm Bay, and there are no roads of any kind there. You have to take a boat or seaplane from Porpoise Bay. Peter Light moved to Storm Bay in the late 1960s, intent on pioneer life. He was the first to build on the little shelf of land, which lies under a great tall cliff. For years he lived there year-round with his family, gardening, homebrewing, and hauling water. They tried to be as self-sufficient as possible, and did it all on a budget of about $12 per month. There was a sweatlodge by the hand-built shack, and a ropeswing out back. The Light kids, Shad and River, didn't go to school until they were aged ten and twelve. Storm Bay kids were different somehow. More trusting. As the community grew, there was communal childcare. A long-ago visitor remembers how one small child hurt her foot, and turned to him, a perfect stranger, for comfort.

In summer, the Light family was joined by painters, dancers, filmmakers, and others, all intent on retreat and warm weather. New houses were put up along the beach, until they numbered ten or so. People gathered in the communal building. Out on Rosehip Point, Flakey

Rosehips summered in his teepee. Nearly everyone wandered around naked, which attracted loggers in low-flying floatplanes, as well as a yearly drug raid from the RCMP. Every year, someone spotted the RCMP boat coming in the distance, and warned the community.

At first, only Peter Light's name was on the land title. One night, when a friend of his was in jail, Peter cavalierly offered the title in place of bail. The Storm Bay folks were alarmed. They called in a lawyer, Peter Fraser. The dancer Karen Jamieson had a great idea: they would put all seventeen members' names on the title. That way, since they would need all seventeen signatures for a decision, they could never lose the land. And once the Storm Bay Joint Tenants Association had been formed, you couldn't make any profit from the place either, since the owners' agreement stipulated that members could only take out what they put in, irrespective of market value (the initial share cost about $1,000).

It's a way of life that still persists today. In summertime, the dark halls of the Western Front are empty. All up and down the coast, Vancouver's artists are basking on driftwood, weeding the garden, raiding the vegetable patch, soaking their tanned limbs in outdoor bathtubs, and nursing glasses of homemade blackberry wine as the sun goes down. They plan their autumn pieces, poems, and performances. As night falls, they sit down to dinner with friends. It's a rich life for poor people, made possible by the collective.

Ecotopia?

Then in your opinion, an orchard is not exactly a garden of Eden?
Not in England, at any rate.
Is it so anywhere – in any part of the world?
Yes: in Canada. At least, so I am told. I mean in British Columbia …
– Julian Ralph, *On Canada's Frontier*

SOMEWHERE ON THE COAST, on a forested land co-op, a battle is raging. One of the members has cut trees on common land, and since there are no written rules about this, the co-op is in an uproar. Members have divided into two camps that volley insults back and forth. They polarize. One side wants no trees cut, period. And no trees trimmed either. No underbrush touched. The others want liberal cutting rights, to open up their views, or make way for new projects. One side grumbles: "These people want to turn this place into Fantasy Gardens!" Stung, the others snap back: "Tree-huggers!" At press time, no compromise had been reached.

The players in that drama are closer than they appear. But their smaller battle quickly takes on the terms of the larger battle raging in our

province, and the famous polarization of British Columbia politics quickly clones itself on smaller stages. Two gardening aesthetics are at war here. The first of these finds its ultimate cartoonish expression in Bill Vander Zalm's Fantasy Gardens, the second in Clayoquot and its peace camp. Fantasy Gardens, the theme-park approach to white settlement in B.C., simply bulldozes what came before. Clayoquot represents the more complicated problem of coming to terms with the history of settlement, and of ecological context.

It seems we have reached the limits of the frontier. We can no longer simply expand into "nowhere," that imagined limitlessness of the north, clearcutting endlessly into an endlessly unrolling landscape. Even the loggers acknowledge it – there are few trees left for the cutting. At the cutting rates that have recently prevailed, no more than fifteen years' worth, perhaps. But given the fact that we are here, what are we to do?

Stuck in the false dichotomy of loggers versus environmentalists, we tend to forget that forestry has not always been dictated by MacMillan Bloedel. In their 1994 book on logging and forestry alternatives, *Forestopia*, Michael M'Gonigle and Ben Parfitt imagine a British Columbia free of the present deadlock. Many people believe that the answer lies in smaller-scale operations.

The story of Ruskin, a turn-of-the-century co-operative mill, is instructive. Ruskin, in the Fraser Valley, was named for the nineteenth-century utopian socialist art critic, John Ruskin. The community began as a Ruskin discussion group, organized by Charles Whetham, who became the principal of Whetham College, an arts college in Vancouver which was a forerunner of the University of B.C.[1] The group of young socialists became inspired to form a settlement organized around a communally owned mill. The company itself was called the Canadian Co-operative Society. The members acquired four acres on the Stave River, which would float logs downstream to the mill. It was incorporated in 1895, and the rules were drawn up in 1896. Ruskin himself, in reaction against the horrors wrought in England by the Industrial Revolution, advocated the

FACING PAGE: *Two men sitting on the porch of one of the original Ruskin commune buildings, 1910. It had in the meantime become a barber shop.*

renunciation of machinery. The CCS couldn't do this, however, since the sawmill was the community centrepiece.

The community members, many of them drawn from the Mission area, were highly idealistic. The co-op would serve to improve them in every way, since "the objects" of their society were to "engage in every branch of lawful industry on the principle of association and the elevation morally and intellectually of its members." While the men worked in the mill, the women worked in the communal garden. Ruskin had its own general store, and a community school. Unfortunately, the school-children could not concentrate on their school work because the mill was too noisy, so the school had to be moved onto Charles Whetham's private land nearby.

Life was good at Ruskin, and so was business. Members were paid a dollar a day. A portion of the weekly payment was issued as a scrip, redeemable at the general store. Business was growing, but the CCS lacked the money to survive the least setback. When the Stave River dried up one particularly hot summer, and logs queued up, Ruskin began to crumble. It hadn't the resources to get through one dry summer. The CCS folded in 1898, and in 1899 it surrendered its assets to E.H. Heaps & Co., which operated a number of mills in the area.

THE RISE AND FALL OF RUSKIN demonstrates more than just the importance of sufficient start-up capital. Such stories may help us to think our way out of the present economic/environmental dilemma over logging. It is clear that we must leave behind left/right dichotomizing. Utopianism, which ultimately transcends the ghettoes of right and left and technology versus ecology, comes in handy here. The richness of utopian history in British Columbia offers countless images of alternative models, ideas, and opportunities. We are reminded of the existence of other dreams which stand outside our present dualism. The uncritical scientific optimism of the Technocracy movement, for example, had its own peculiar logic. Founded in the fertile primeval swamp of the inter-war era, Technocracy placed all its hopes for humanity in technological progress. Its Kingsway headquarters in Burnaby, where Technocrats assembled for weekly lectures, retained its 1930s feel over the decades, until it finally closed down in 1993.

Technocracy found itself echoed in Walden Two, a scientific utopia built by Vernon Pick near Lillooet. The RCMP investigated Walden Two in 1975 after locals became convinced that Pick, a self-made American millionaire, was building a private nuclear arms base. What they found were the building blocks of a technological paradise – a richly appointed compound with chandeliers and libraries well-stocked with Thoreau, encircled by a woodworking shop, a machine shop, a laboratory, an electric railway, a dam, and a power plant. There were landscaped gardens and smooth green lawns, as well as a pond – named for Walden Pond. All it needed was people. Pick, who made his first $10 million from a uranium claim, began dreaming his independent community while reading Thoreau. But its resemblance to Walden ended with self-sufficiency.

The primary purpose of Pick's first community, Walden West, built in California, was electronics research. He envisioned the same thing for Walden North: himself at the centre of a humming society of technical workers and thinkers. "What we must do," he is quoted as saying, "is look to the future and try to improve it."[2]

In 1975, Walden North was empty save for Pick, his wife, and his nephew, a bearded machinist who had left his job in the United States to live at Walden. Before he could fill the place with worker bees, Pick became bored and moved away – unsurprisingly, perhaps, since Walden North was fuelled by his enthusiasm alone. Ten years later the complex was up for sale, with an asking price of $3.4 million. It had sat silent for some years by then, a sleeping giant, waiting for morning. The multimillionaire Jimmy Pattison got a tour of the place, and seriously considered buying it. Vernon Pick, meanwhile, had set his sights on Switzerland. A new Walden was in the works.

Worlds away, as Pick was busy building his Waldens, the environ-

Vernon Pick, 1974: a man among his machines.

mental movement was gaining speed. British Columbia was rife with activism. The province has been a hotbed of environmental thinking for ages: Greenpeace originated in Vancouver in 1971, when a small group of protesters chartered a fishing boat, the *Phyllis Cormack*, to go and protest nuclear testing off Alaska. The Greenpeacers made a quick convert of John Cormack, the owner of the boat. He began by dismissing them as a lot of mad hippies, and ended on Greenpeace's board of directors. Paul Watson's interventionist group, the Sea Shepherd Conservation Society, was an early offshoot. And then there was Habitat Forum, the alternative to the United Nations conference on human habitation, held at Jericho Beach in 1976. Some inspiration came from Ernest Callenbach's didactic novel, *Ecotopia* (1975), which depicts the Pacific Northwest, including northern California, as the low-tech promised land of the future. In Callenbach's world, North America has been rearranged along aboriginal lines, its borders drawn longitudinally. It is a society organized by environmentalism. The Ecotopians organize their lives along sound ecological principles, recycling and relying on assorted forms of natural energy. But Callenbach is a rather graceless novelist, so his ecological lessons weigh down the narrative. *Ecotopia* is primarily a vehicle, a means of spreading ideas and practical suggestions. As such, it does offer something to the history of alternatives.

For Krishna Kumar, the author of *Utopia and Anti-Utopia in Modern Times* (1987), "ecotopia" denotes a whole contemporary strain of anarchist-inspired environmentalism which aims for a balance between 1960s idealism and the informed pessimism of later decades, between what was hoped for and what was learned. Can ecological principles be grafted with technological expertise to form a new economy for B.C.?

Some people see a happy marriage in the present-day pot farms of the Kootenays, where many communes have evolved into large-scale marijuana farms, making money for the community and millionaires out of the old hippies. Things have changed since the late 1960s, when the locals hated and feared the longhairs. The column "Tribes" used to serve as a clearing house for warnings: back-to-the-landers sent warnings for fellow hippies – watch out for such-and-such a place; they'll pull guns in such-and-such a bar. But today those same hippies are appreciated for their community spirit. They put a lot of money into community projects, money made possible by technical advances in growing methods. They care about the towns themselves, and they need the goodwill of the other residents. It's a symbiotic relationship. And communes and collectives can grow to form an extended family, or safety net, in the lean times we all anticipate.

The utopian impulse still beats strong in British Columbia, and it is limited neither to survivors nor to neo-hippies like the Circling Dawn Organic Foods Collective, with its organic squash and summer teepees. Assorted plans continue to percolate – an intentional community on Vancouver Island, for example, by the people who brought us Capers. In another vein, communities of squatting street people ("shrubbies") have sprung up unregulated in the woods of Hornby and other Gulf Islands. These experiments are varied in nature, and that is part of their virtue.

If utopian culture has a function, it is to top up the cup of possibility. All too often, history is presented as a homogeneous mass, and events seem to unfold mechanically, as though there were only ever one possible outcome, which is "the way things are." To many people, a heavy, bleak future seems inevitable. But the utopian record, with its assorted outcomes, presents a number of detours. The history of utopias suggests other models and other scenarios for a possible British Columbia. They remind us not of how life should be, but rather how it might be.

Sources & Acknowledgments

THIS BOOK GREW OUT OF MEMORY and a study of utopian fiction. My sources include personal interviews and archival material, as well as published histories of individual communities. I use the Cambridge edition of Sir Thomas More's *Utopia*, edited by George M. Logan and Robert M. Adams (New York: Cambridge University Press, 1989). Peter Sloterdijk's *Critique of Cynical Reason* (Minneapolis: University of Minnesota Press, 1987) was inspirational.

The cover shows a stage backdrop painted by Sointulans in the 1930s; it hangs in the Sointula Museum today. John Oliphant, King and Cindy Anderson, and Bob Sarti were kind enough to provide photographs. Other photos should be credited as follows: p. 6, British Columbia Archives and Records Service No. 72143; p. 16, BCARS 1287; p. 19, BCARS 68354; p. 22, BCARS 95349; p. 30, UBC Special Collections; p. 34, Vancouver Public Library No. 13057; p. 47, Ian Lindsay/*Vancouver Sun*; p. 50, VPL 7923; pp. 54-55, VPL 186; p. 57, BCARS 55359; p. 62, Steve Hodgson; p. 78, King Anderson; p. 86, VPL 13050; p. 89, Brian Kent/*Vancouver Sun*.

Thanks: to Taras Grescoe, for everything. To Terry Glavin and Rolf Maurer, for everything else. To George Brandak at University of B.C. Special Collections, for pointing me to the James Bowman papers. To Tom, for the memories of New Denver. To all the people who talked to me and gave me photos. To my mother, Joan Haggerty, for taking me there. And to Donal, the first listener.

I REMEMBER UTOPIA

1. James Bowman wrote an article, partly using solicited material, which gives

a brief overview of the history of utopian or "intentional" communities in this province. He discusses Sointula and the Doukhobors as well as more contemporary examples such as the Emissaries and CEEDS. See "Historical Notes on Intentional Communities in B.C." in *Communities* 36 (January/February 1979), p. 36. It is the only overview of the subject that I have come across.

2. See my article "Phantasia: Utopian Communities in B.C. Fiction" in the Spring 1996 issue of *BC Studies* for a fuller exploration of the literary side of the question.

3. See Jean Barman's book of this title (Toronto: University of Toronto Press, 1991) for for a good overview of B.C. history.

4. Brenda Lea White quotes Nicol in her introduction to a collection she edited, *British Columbia: Visions of the Promised Land* (Vancouver: Flight Press, 1986).

METLAKATLA

1. The phrase belongs to Howard White. I am indebted to his "Bringing the Indians to Their Knees [Metlakatla]" in *Raincoast Chronicles First Five* (Madeira Park: Harbour, 1976), as well as Peter Murray's *The Devil and Mr. Duncan* (Victoria: Sono Nis, 1985) for most of the material for this chapter.

NORTHERN LIGHTS

1. Cliff Kopas, *Bella Coola* (Vancouver: J.J. Douglas, 1970). Other sources include Iver Fougner's "The Founding of Bella Coola" in a 1904 issue of *The Canadian Magazine*, and Gordon Fish's *Dreams of Freedom: Bella Coola, Cape Scott, Sointula* (Victoria: Provincial Archives Sound Heritage Series, 1982). See also Lester R. Peterson, *The Cape Scott Story* (Langley: Sunfire, 1985).

2. Scott Lawrance, "Sointula: Salt Fish and Spuds Utopia," in *Raincoast Chronicles First Five*.

3. Allan Henry Salo's 1978 UBC M.A. thesis, "The Kalevan Kansa Colonization Company, Ltd.: A Finnish Canadian Millenarian Movement in B.C.," is an intriguing source for material on Sointula. Salo quotes at length from *Aika*.

PROSPERO'S ISLANDS

1. Susan Musgrave's Chela character in her novel *The Charcoal Burners* (1980) also owes something to Brother Twelve. The novel is, among other things, a bitterly sarcastic dirge for 1960s-inspired utopianism. The Chela, the cannibal-commune leader, is a carny figure who creates a magical persona. The term chela, meaning initiate or master, was current among theosophists.

2. See Herbert Emmerson Wilson, *Canada's False Prophet: The Notorious Brother Twelve* (Richmond Hill: Simon & Schuster, 1967). This Wilson appears

to have been a charlatan of a different stripe. Herbert, a circuit preacher and ex-con, lived on a houseboat outside Ladysmith. He probably heard the stories from colonists and is said to have hired ghostwriter Thomas P. Kelley to produce the book. See Peter Trower's "The Temptations of a Safe-cracking Preacher" in *Vancouver Magazine* (July 1982). The latest and most authoritative book on the subject is by John Oliphant, *Brother Twelve: The Incredible Story of Canada's False Prophet* (Toronto: McClelland & Stewart, 1991).

3. There have been all kinds of colonies on the Gulf Islands over the years. As early as 1859, Saltspring Island became home to a group of black colonists from California, who left the state when a series of racially discriminatory laws were passed in 1858. Governor James Douglas extended them a cordial invitation (there was a labour shortage in Victoria). The San Francisco Emigrant Society declared "Vancouver's Island" "a place which has unfolded to us in our darkest hour, the prospect of a bright future." About four hundred blacks came, travelling together. Some stayed in Victoria, and some were siphoned off by the gold rush, but a sizeable group settled on Saltspring. The colony was not strictly utopian, but united nonetheless by flight and by a desire for freedom. The colonists were also united by fear: having settled the northwest end of the island, they were right across from the Kuper Island village of Penelakut, where a disaffected band of native pirates had their base. But diarists elaborate the sense of Gulf-Island-as-refuge. Food – game, clams, fish, berries – was naturally abundant. Life was hard but good. Many blacks returned to the United States after the Civil War, but the descendants of others still live on Saltspring today.

4. Ronald MacIsaac, *The Brother XII: Devil of De Courcy Island* (Victoria: Press Porcépic, 1989).

5. Allan Edmonds' first piece, "Would You Give Up $25,000 a Year to Find 'Peace' Doing Chores in an Island Commune?" appeared in *Maclean's* (August, 1970). The companion piece, "Paradise Lost," appeared in the May, 1991 issue of *West*.

6. Tim Gallagher, "Sex, Drugs, and Religious Icons," *British Columbia Report*, May 6, 1991. See also assorted articles by Moira Farrow in the *Vancouver Sun* (April 30, 1991; November 5, 1991; June 9, 1993; December 3, 1994).

SPIRIT WRESTLING

1. Jim Carrico, who grew up near Pemberton in the 1960s, remarks that in his school "Doukhobor" was bandied about like a racial epithet (i.e., "Hey, ya Doukhobor! … That guy called me a Doukhobor, man … ," etc.).

2. See the informative history *The Doukhobors* by George Woodcock and Ivan Avakumovic (Toronto: Oxford University Press, 1968). This book went a long way to illuminating what had come to be known as "the Doukhobor problem" in Canada, and promoted an objective yet more positive image of the group.

Most of the material for this chapter comes from this book.

3. C.P. Anderson, ed. *Circle of Voices: A History of the Religious Communities of B.C.* (Lantzville: Oolichan, 1983), p. 115.

4. Elsie G. Turnbull, *Ghost Towns and Drowned Towns of the West Kootenay* (Surrey: Heritage House, 1988).

RIVAL WORLDS

1. Mark Vonnegut, *The Eden Express* (New York: Bantam, 1974), p. 9.

2. Terry Allan Simmons, *But We Must Cultivate Our Garden: Twentieth Century Pioneering in Rural British Columbia* (Minneapolis: University of Minnesota Press, 1979), p. 217.

3. Anderson, ed., *Circle of Voices*, p. 164.

4. The Argenta Friends School (AFS) represents the avant-garde of the alternate-school movement in British Columbia, setting the stage for numerous "free schools" like the New School in Vancouver and Helen Hughes' Windsor House in North Vancouver, which she founded so that her daughter, Meghan, would have a liberated education. AFS graduate Dave Gregg, who attended in the 1970s, remembers that most school decisions were taken by consensus: students were viewed as equal participants.

5. I have found James Bowman's papers, a collection of material on intentional communities in UBC's Special Collections, to be indispensable. They contain most issues of *Open Circle* and the CEEDS newsletter, *In Defense of Nature*, as well as important issues of *Communities* magazine. Bowman also included a lot of important correspondence between members on a number of practical and theoretical topics.

6. *B.C. Access Catalogue* (Vancouver, 1974).

7. Chris Foster, *One Heart, One Way: The Life and Legacy of Martin Exeter* (Denver, Co.: Foundation House, 1989), p. 147.

LOWRY'S LEGACY

1. Malcolm Lowry, *October Ferry to Gabriola* (New York: World Publishing, 1970), p. 62.

2. *Vancouver Sun*, June 28, 1971.

3. "Sunshine Coast communes arouse local ire," *Vancouver Sun*, June 28, 1971.

ECOTOPIA

1. Sheila Nickols, ed. *Maple Ridge: A History of Settlement* (Maple Ridge: Canadian Federation of University Women, 1972), p. 52.

2. *Vancouver Sun*, January 23, 1975.

Published by New Star Books Ltd. All rights reserved. No part of this work may be repro-
duced or used in any form or by any means – graphic, electronic, or mechanical –
without prior permission. Any request for photocopying or other reprographic copying
must be sent in writing to the Canadian Copyright Licensing Agency (CANCOPY), 900 - 6
Adelaide Street East, Toronto, Ontario M5C 1H6

Please direct submissions and editorial enquiries to: Transmontanus, Box C-25, Fernhill
Road, Mayne Island, B.C. V0N 2J0. All other correspondence, including sales and distri-
bution enquiries, should be directed to New Star Books, 2504 York Avenue, Vancouver,
B.C. V6K 1E3

Transmontanus is edited by Terry Glavin
Series design by Val Speidel
Cover photograph by Connie Rock
Author photograph by Diyah Pera
Produced by Rolf Maurer and Val Speidel
Printed and bound in Canada by Best Book Manufacturers
1 2 3 4 5   99 98 97 96 95

Production of this book is made possible by grants from the Canada Council and the
Cultural Services Branch, Province of British Columbia

CATALOGUING IN PUBLICATION DATA
    Brown, Justine, 1965-
    All possible worlds

    (Transmontanus, ISSN 1200-3336; v. 5)
    Includes bibliographical references.
    ISBN 0-921586-46-9
    1. Utopias – British Columbia – History. 2. Collective settlements – British
Columbia – History. 3. British Columbia – Social conditions. I. Title. II. Series.
HX659.B7B7 1995   335'.02'0971109   C95-911018-6